Blake J. Neff, PhD

A Pastor's Guide to Interpersonal Communication
The Other Six Days

D1596536

More pre-publication
REVIEWS, COMMENTARIES, EVALUATIONS . . .

"Dr. Neff has united the academic with the practical for a very readable journey through actual case studies that will give you opportunities to gain wisdom from his research. This book provides a source of reference for those of us engaged in the high calling of doing ministry. It is a must-read to help us gain insights to the various life experiences we all face or will face. The charts and graphs allow us to think through the maze of variables that accompany each crisis."

Mel Truex, ThB, MEd
Senior Pastor,
Faith Memorial Church,
Lancaster, Ohio

"What a helpful, practical book for pastors on the things we may have never learned in our training!"

Keith Drury, MRe, DD, LHD
Associate Professor
of Practical Ministry,
Indiana Wesleyan University;
Weekly Column posted at
http://www.DruryWriting.com/keith

"Pastors and church councils will find *A Pastoral Guide to Interpersonal Communication* a very helpful resource. This book will assist members of the church council in realizing the vast amount of time spent by pastors in interpersonal communication and the complexity of those communications. The pastor will find abundant practical tools to develop better interpersonal communication skills. Utilizing pastoral conversations with analysis questions, Pastor Neff creates the setting for lively interpersonal communication with the reader. To assist the reader in understanding and implementing these concepts, he ends each chapter with a summary of key concepts, a glossary, and practical homework suggestions for unleashing the power of interpersonal communication. This repetitive summarizing technique also aids in modeling vital interpersonal communication. As well organized and comprehensive as this book is, it is the discussion of dual relationships which captures this reviewer. While clergy and parishioners all recognize the presence of dual relationships, few works even treat the subject. Pastor Neff provides a frank and succinct treatment as well as healthy guidelines for dealing with this important area of dual relationships and interpersonal communication. Unafraid, he tackles five controversial areas: pastor as counselor, as lover, as friend, as family member, and as former pastor. In discussing the dangers and strengths of dual relationships, Pastor Neff has done a great service for pastors and their communities of faith."

Dr. Bill Vermillion, MDiv, PhD
General Superintendent,
Evangelical Church of North America

A Pastor's Guide
to Interpersonal
Communication
The Other Six Days

THE HAWORTH PASTORAL PRESS®
Haworth Series in Chaplaincy
Andrew J. Weaver, MTh, PhD
Editor

Living Faithfully with Disappointment in the Church by J. LeBron McBride

Young Clergy: A Biographical-Developmental Study by Donald Capps

Grief, Loss, and Death: The Shadow Side of Ministry by Halbert Weidner

Prison Ministry: Hope Behind the Wall by Dennis W. Pierce

A Pastor's Guide to Interpersonal Communication: The Other Six Days by Blake J. Neff

Pastoral Care of Depression: Helping Clients Heal Their Relationship with God by Glendon Moriarty

Pastoral Care with Younger Adults in Long-Term Care by Reverend Jacqueline Sullivan

The Spirituality of Community Life: When We Come 'Round Right by Ronald P. McDonald

Pastoral Care from the Pulpit: Meditations of Hope and Encouragement by J. LeBron McBride

A Pastor's Guide to Interpersonal Communication
The Other Six Days

Blake J. Neff, PhD

The Haworth Pastoral Press®
An Imprint of The Haworth Press, Inc.
New York • London • Oxford

For more information on this book or to order, visit
http://www.haworthpress.com/store/product.asp?sku=5388

or call 1-800-HAWORTH (800-429-6784) in the United States and Canada
or (607) 722-5857 outside the United States and Canada

or contact orders@HaworthPress.com

Published by

The Haworth Pastoral Press®, an imprint of The Haworth Press, Inc., 10 Alice Street, Binghamton,
NY 13904-1580.

PUBLISHER'S NOTE
The development, preparation, and publication of this work has been undertaken with great care.
However, the Publisher, employees, editors, and agents of The Haworth Press are not responsible
for any errors contained herein or for consequences that may ensue from use of materials or
information contained in this work. The Haworth Press is committed to the dissemination of ideas
and information according to the highest standards of intellectual freedom and the free exchange of
ideas. Statements made and opinions expressed in this publication do not necessarily reflect the
views of the Publisher, Directors, management, or staff of The Haworth Press, Inc., or an
endorsement by them.

Unless otherwise noted, all Bible verses are from the New International Version (NIV). Copyright
1973, 1978, 1984 by International Bible Society. Used by permission of Zondervan. All rights
reserved.

Cover design by Jennifer M. Gaska.

Library of Congress Cataloging-in-Publication Data

Neff, Blake J.
A pastor's guide to interpersonal communication : the other six days / Blake J. Neff.
    p. cm.
Includes bibliographical references and index.
ISBN-13: 978-0-7890-2665-1 (hc. : alk. paper)
ISBN-10: 0-7890-2665-1 (hc. : alk. paper)
ISBN-13: 978-0-7890-2666-8 (pbk. : alk. paper)
ISBN-10: 0-7890-2666-X (pbk. : alk. paper)
    1. Pastoral theology. 2. Interpersonal communication—Religious aspects—Christianity. I.
Title.

BV4319.N44 2006
253'.7—dc22
                                                                                    2005024815

CONTENTS

Preface

I cannot recall where I first heard the line. I do know, however, that for more than twenty-five years it has proven invaluable. Not only does utterance of my trademark phrase always gain a laugh, it usually helps me gain perspective. The fact that it comes out of the mouth of a member of the clergy only intensifies the line's great value in the sight of others. The line?

"I love humanity; it's just people I can't stand."

The expression is so versatile. I find it appropriate when

> Another driver cuts into my lane on the highway.
>
> The appliance repairperson fails to show up when promised, even though I stayed home all day to wait.
>
> A hotel clerk assigns me to a room not yet visited by maid service after the previous night's guests.
>
> The phone company's prerecorded representative insists, "We're sorry, your call cannot be completed as dialed."

But, "I love humanity; it's just people I can't stand," is a line not just for the secular world. The line also has limitless value for use in the church. For example, when

> The Sunday school superintendent tells a visiting family that we really don't have room for any new children in the Sunday school.
>
> The board chairperson announces a change to less frequent board meetings in the midst of a major building campaign, because she or he is just burned out on church meetings.
>
> The church matriarch shouts "amen" when it is announced that the choir will not be singing next Sunday.

A thirty-year church veteran announces that he or she will not
attend any more services until the pastor moves because there
are far too many altar calls.

An elderly saint declares that he or she will not be attending any
more services until the pastor moves because there are not
enough altar calls.

In short, in the church or outside it is just easier to love humanity
than to love the individual people that make up that humanity. This
may be one of the reasons why Bible colleges, Christian liberal arts
preministry programs, and theological seminaries specialize in the
love of humanity. The result is that many pastors really do love people, but they have little experience or information with regard to how
to demonstrate that love. They are not skilled in the development and
maintenance of relationships.

FEATURES

A Pastor's Guide to Interpersonal Communication focuses on the
real people of the church, as well as the art of loving and demonstrat-
ing love to them. It applies the best techniques available in interpersonal communication to the real world of the sometimes unlovable
people in the church. The text is comprehensive, exploring how communication works and the basic tools of the communicator. But, the
text also delves into such topics as listening, managing conflict, per-
suading, forgiving, and utilizing interpersonal power. The ethics of
pastoral interpersonal communication are explored in a special chapter on dual relationships, while primary relationships comprise the
topic of the final chapter.

Throughout the text, "Pastoral Conversations" provide emphasis
and opportunities for analysis. Although names and circumstances
have been substantially altered in order to protect the confidentiality
of others, many of these cases have their origin in real-life pastoral
situations.

In addition, each chapter offers the student the opportunity to revisit central truths through "Key Concepts," which summarize the
important points. Also, "Meanings Mania" provides a vocabulary
matching exercise. These two features combine to provide a unique
approach to summary and review.

"Unleashing the Power of Interpersonal Communication" provides an exercise for each chapter. These learning activities are designed to incorporate the principles of the chapter with an opportunity to practice people skills in an interpersonal setting. The result is a hands-on approach to interpersonal communication.

ABOUT THE AUTHOR

Blake J. Neff, MTh, PhD, is pastor of the Van Buren United Methodist Church in Van Buren, Indiana, and an adjunct faculty member at Indiana Wesleyan University in Marion. He previously served as President of Vennard College in University Park, Iowa, and Director of the School of Communication at Toccoa Falls College in Toccoa Falls, Georgia.

Dr. Neff is the co-author of *The Complete Guide to Religious Education Volunteers* and *Sunday Ethic, Monday World,* and co-editor of the *Handbook of Family Religious Education.*

Acknowledgments

This book would not be possible without the loving support of my chief supporter and confidant, Nancy. Together we have ministered interpersonally and professionally to a combined total of more than a thousand church members over the past twenty-seven years. She is far better at loving people. I still prefer humanity.

Nor would this book be possible without those church members and attendees who have been our laboratory rats in a long-term relational experiment. Some, who already know who they are, have become especially dear. To all we offer grateful appreciation.

A special word of appreciation is offered to Tracy Thurman, whose artistic abilities are well known around Van Buren United Methodist Church. Her original artwork in Figures 3.2 and 7.1 are much appreciated.

Thank you for reading *A Pastor's Guide to Interpersonal Communication*. Whether you have the book in your hand by choice, or because a professor said you must, my prayer is the same. "And this is my prayer: that your love may abound more and more . . ." (Philippians 1:9). Of course I mean your love for both humanity and people.

Chapter 1

Interpersonal Pastoral Communication

Several pastors in a small-town community ministerial association agreed to keep a weekly log of time spent in ministry to share with the others. The idea was to create an accountability group designed to develop more effective ministry. When one member presented his log, he insisted that he consistently spent more than 110 hours per week in his pastoral work. All but time he spent sleeping appeared on the log. "Whether I like it or not, every waking hour, I am the pastor," he boastfully declared.

"What about this large block of time each afternoon watching television?" a colleague queried suspiciously.

"I get valuable sermon illustrations from the afternoon soaps," came the immediate, straight-faced response.

Most pastors would question the idea that pastoral ministry includes watching soap operas, or involves 110 hours a week. Yet conscientious pastors do spend a great deal of time at their work, and a large portion of that time is spent in nonpublic endeavors. Major pastoral responsibilities include prayer, Bible reading, devotional study, sermon preparation, and other activities conducted in solitude.

In addition, pastors spend numerous hours in interpersonal, one-on-one settings. Building relationships, discussing church business, making shut-in calls, welcoming newcomers, offering counsel, engaging in evangelism, and mentoring new disciples are all a part of the typical pastor's busy workweek.

Parishioners may not realize the amount of time their pastor invests in these kinds of either private or dyadic endeavors. Such is the case in Pastoral Conversation 1.1. Although Pastor Southerland is very conscientious about his ministry, at least one parishioner does not understand the pastor's workload.

Pastoral Conversation 1.1

Background

Shawn and Greg, two members of Harmony Community Church who serve on the Staff Parish Committee, are seated in the corner booth of Dana's Café. It is 7:00 a.m. on a Tuesday. The pair met, as they do each day, for a cup of coffee on the way to work. This morning the conversation turns naturally to last night's Staff Parish Committee meeting.

Dialogue

SHAWN: It's always a tough meeting in the fall when we have to recommend next year's pastoral salary to the Administrative Committee.

GREG: I thought we would never get everyone to agree.

SHAWN: The five percent increase in salary that we settled on is fair, though.

GREG: I'm not so sure, Shawn. I can't help but think about the total package. With the increase we approved, Pastor Southerland will make almost as much as I do.

SHAWN: What's wrong with that? He has invested a great deal of time and money in education. He has nearly twenty years of experience. Besides, I think he preaches an excellent sermon.

GREG: No argument from me there. His sermons are interesting to listen to and spiritually challenging. In fact, I credit Pastor Southerland's preaching with the reason Harmony Church is growing.

SHAWN: So what's the problem?

GREG: It's just that I have to work at least five and sometimes six days a week to make that kind of money. What does Pastor Southerland do the other six days?

SHAWN: (with a mischievous grin) Here comes Pastor Southerland now. Why don't you ask him?

Analysis

1. How would you answer Greg's question about what Pastor Southerland does Monday through Saturday?
2. Is Greg's concern about Pastor Southerland's workload reasonable? What is the evidence for your response?
3. What are the differences between Pastor Southerland's Sunday ministry and his Monday through Saturday ministry? How do these differences lead to Greg's concerns?
4. If Greg and Shawn were to raise the issue with Pastor Southerland, how would you recommend he respond?

Greg's concern that Pastor Southerland works only one day a week for a full-time salary is not uncommon. People tend to only recognize what they experience personally. Since their direct exposure to their pastor is often limited to Sunday morning, they subconsciously assume that Sunday morning is the extent of a pastor's responsibility. By contrast most pastors report that Sunday morning activities encompass only a small percentage of their total ministry time.

A survey conducted by George Barna (1993) of the Barna Research Group reveals that pastors spend an average of only three hours per week in worship. Rainer (2001) discovered similar results. After identifying and surveying "effective" pastors, he reports that this group spends about five hours per week in worship activities.

Laypeople who see the pastor only those three to five hours per week may assume the pastor spends the rest of his or her time watching afternoon television or engaged in other frivolous pursuits. They may therefore ask, "What does the pastor do with the rest of the forty hours that constitute a normal workweek for me?"

Of course most laypeople, upon deeper consideration, would graciously acknowledge the fact that preparation for Sunday morning requires several hours of pastoral time each week. The pastors in the Barna study report spending only ten hours per week in sermon preparation. Rainer's effective pastors spent a much more significant twenty-two hours per week in that activity.

In addition, in the Barna survey pastors reported spending eight hours each week in administrative work and committee meetings. Rainer's effective pastors spend more time in administration, averaging fifteen hours on such tasks. As a result, those laypeople who are involved in the administrative life of the church would be much more likely to see their pastor's activity in this important area. Hence, Shawn may well respond to Greg in the follow-up to Pastoral Conversation 1.1, "I know what Pastor Southerland does with several more hours each week, because I work alongside him at many of those same committee meetings and planning sessions."

But, what neither Greg nor Shawn are likely to recognize are the many hours Pastor Southerland spends in one-on-one ministry. They, and their lay colleagues, have no way of knowing that the average pastor utilizes five hours per week for visitation, two hours for counseling, two hours in evangelism, and an additional two hours discipling people; a total of eleven hours in interpersonal communication activities (Barna, 1993). Rainer discovered that effective church leaders spend ten hours per week doing pastoral care including counseling, visitation, weddings, and funerals. In addition, they spend five hours per week in personal evangelism and five hours per week mentoring. This is a total of twenty hours in a typical workweek engaged in one-on-one activities.

A major portion of the answer to the question, "What does a pastor do all week?" involves interpersonal relationships and dyadic communication. Yet in spite of the large blocks of time pastors spend in dyadic communication, many feel inadequately prepared for that part of their ministry. Barna discovered that only 23 percent of pastors believe they are doing an excellent job in developing relationships. One pastor, who apparently represented the remaining 77 percent, lamented that she had a few courses in seminary on preaching, and countless more on exegesis and other preparations for preaching. She had a course or two in church administration, but never had the first course on communicating with people interpersonally, or in the important area of relationship-building.

Rainer (2001) suggests one possible reason for the interpersonal lack of confidence among pastors when he writes, "Most evangelical seminaries and Bible colleges do at least an adequate job in training pastors in the classical disciplines. Where many institutions fall short, however, is in preparing ministers in preaching, leadership, and interpersonal skills" (p. 68). If Rainer's observation is accurate, pastoral education institutions are offering miniscule training in the area where pastors spend a high percentage of their professional time.

Even those clergy who had one of the courses in interpersonal communication, helping relationships, or peer counseling offered in most college and university undergraduate programs may find the experience less helpful than they had hoped. Often such courses offer general illustrations and applications. The pastor, or pastor in training, finds little by way of specific help in developing or understanding those relationships unique to pastoral ministry. The typical pastor may therefore accept the challenges of a first pastoral assignment with little or no training in the very activity that will encompass the largest block of ministry time.

Johnson (1997) points out that humans are not born knowing how to interact with others. Effective communication is not instantaneous, and relational skills do not appear as if by magic when they are needed. Other experts in interpersonal communication agree that interpersonal skills must be learned and developed through careful study and precise training.

Weaver (1996), in his classic textbook on relationships, maintains that the goal of his book is to help the reader become more effective at sending and receiving interpersonal messages. After each chapter he offers a section entitled, "Improving Skills in Interpersonal Communication." He thus affirms the notion that interpersonal skills are learnable. But the help in Weaver's text supports the relationships of a typical college student, which of course is his target audience. He offers nothing that can be directly applied by those engaged in, or preparing for, the business of pastoral ministry.

Similarly, Veendendall and Feinstein (1996) agree that interpersonal skills can be learned. To that end they offer a chapter on "Communication Competence and Effectiveness." Again, pastors seeking to improve communication competence and effectiveness in pastoral relationships would find the techniques imprecise for their unique setting.

Johnson (1997) also offers a chapter titled, "Increasing Your Communication Skills." He offers advice to communication generalists however, not to pastoral ministers.

KEYS TO IMPROVING INTERPERSONAL SKILLS

The unique area of pastoral relationships remains unmentioned by each of these authors, yet a compilation of the teachings of these and other communication experts reveals several key ways by which interpersonal competence can be improved. With appropriate adaptation, these keys become instructional to those involved in pastoral ministry.

Key 1: Develop New Relationships

Weaver (1996) suggests that those interested in becoming more effective communicators should actively search out new relationships. People should not shy away from potential encounters just because they appear to be unlike what they have been involved with in the past. For the pastor this advice obviously includes building relationships outside the parish.

Pastor Martin developed a vital friendship with a local businessperson who was active in another congregation. The relationship broadened the pastor's understanding of business matters and provided church-related insights from a layperson's point of view. At the same time, Pastor Martin avoided the ethical pitfalls that are often associated with developing close personal friendships within the congregation. (See Chapter 13.)

Other pastors find colleagues in ministry become a rich source of friendship in addition to providing a professional support group. Considering colleagues in ministry to be "new relationships," however, limits the pastor's development in a second important key to improvement of interpersonal skills.

Key 2: Develop New Interests

Often relationships with other pastors become primarily a matter of "talking shop." Although such relationships may be fulfilling, they seldom provide the kind of broad exposure to new interests that improve interpersonal communication competence. Instead, pastors benefit from seeking exposure to persons and ideas outside the realm of theology, pastoral care, or church administration. Reading outside one's field is one way to help develop new interests, as is participation in self-improvement classes such as those offered in many communities at the library or YMCA.

Pastor Nikki developed both new interests and new relationships when she joined the volunteer emergency medical technicians (EMTs) in her community. An important serendipity was the opportunity to assist people from her own community who were in the midst of physical, life-and-death situations. An interesting note: Pastor Nikki resisted encouragement by others in the group to become the organization's chaplain. "That would not have been expanding my interpersonal exposures," she noted. "I would just have been in the same role, but transferred to a different setting."

Key 3: Metacommunicate

Communication specialists use the term metacommunication when they refer to communication about communication. Effectiveness as an interpersonal communicator often depends upon a person's willingness to utilize metacommunication. Effective interpersonal communicators do not allow doubts to persist about another person's meaning. These practical, dyadic experts metacommunicate in order to eliminate such doubts. Notice Pastor Ron's need to metacommunicate in Pastoral Conversation 1.2.

Pastoral Conversation 1.2

Background

Pastor Ron is greeting parishioners at the door after the morning worship. He has just preached a message that he recognizes is somewhat controversial for some of his parishioners. Freda Poole, a key leader in the church, has stepped up to greet Pastor Ron.

Dialogue

PASTOR RON: So good to see you this morning, Freda.

FREDA: Nice to see you too, Pastor. That was a very interesting message.

Analysis

Since the word *interesting* can be interpreted several ways in this context, Pastor Ron has available at least three optional responses.

Possible Response 1. "Thank you, Freda. I'm glad you appreciated the message."

Possible Response 2. "Thank you for your candor, Freda. I'm sorry you didn't appreciate the message."

Possible Response 3. "I'm not sure I understand what you mean by interesting. Your opinion is very important to me. Would you mind saying more about what you mean?"

The third response invites metacommunication. Clearly it gives Pastor Ron the best opportunity to develop his future relationship with Freda as well as understand what she means in the present situation. With this response he affirms her importance. He also establishes the ineffectiveness of their interpersonal communication in the present dialogue.

On the other hand, as in nearly every case, metacommunication in Pastoral Conversation 1.2 has risks. Of course Freda might accept response 3, Pastor Ron's attempt at metacommunication, at face value. That is, she might think, "The pastor respects my opinion and wants to understand my point of view." But, she may also say to herself, "I tried to be gentle about his poor message, but Pastor Ron just insists on confrontation." Or, if she intended a compliment, she might think, "I offer a compliment, but he is so self-consumed that he insists we go over my comment a second time."

Pastors must be careful with metacommunication. With practice and a genuine willingness to learn from others, they can effectively use this important tool for enhancing interpersonal communication skills.

Key 4: Increase Self-Awareness

Interpersonal relationships require the active and sensitive participation of two people. Often pastors and others trained in the caring professions find it natural to understand the needs, hurts, aspirations, and challenges of others. They may, however, find it less comfortable to comprehend their own emotional makeup. Self-awareness is not the same as self-pity, self-aggrandizement, or selfishness. Instead, self-awareness causes people to recognize both their strengths and their weaknesses. As a result they have the freedom to more carefully follow the injunction of the Apostle Paul, "Do not think of yourself more highly than you ought, but rather think of yourself with sober judgment . . ." (Romans 12:3).

One way to improve self-awareness involves completing a self-profile. The self-profile process includes making candid and comprehensive assessment through a series of self-observations. The ten-item questionnaire in Exhibit 1.1 will serve as a valuable starting point for the pastor or ministerial student interested in developing a self-profile.

EXHIBIT 1.1. Developing a Self-Profile

1. My greatest strength in ministry is _____.

2. My greatest weakness in ministry is _____.

3. When people meet me for the first time they are most likely to notice

   _____.

4. I get most angry at _____.

5. _____ makes me happiest.

6. The things I would be willing to die for are _____.

7. My various roles in addition to pastor are _____.

8. Six adjectives I would use to describe myself and my ministry are:

   _____   _____

   _____   _____

   _____   _____

9. Thus far my greatest joy in ministry has been _____.

10. Thus far my greatest disappointment in ministry has been _____

    _____.

Pastors should recognize that self-concept is subjective, even though some view personal assessment as absolute truth. In reality it may be artificial, partial, or distorted. For example, Belz (2002) recalls inviting a friend to list the top five preachers in the friend's denomination. "You'd have to put me on that list, I think," came the immodest response. Belz notes, "I didn't. Not that day, nor since" (p. 5). Belz's friend obviously needed a huge dose of humility. In addition, the friend's self-awareness apparently would improve with a measure of objective truth.

Researchers have discovered that people are unwilling to alter self-awareness once it has been developed. In fact, many people try to reinforce their present self-concept by seeking out relationships with others who confirm their current self-view (Adler and Towne, 2003). For example, Pastor Edwin reported a large number of home visits in his monthly report to the pulpit committee, but he apparently was using "pseudo" pastoral care to camouflage efforts to boost his self-image. Upon careful scrutiny, the committee concluded that the pastor called frequently in the same homes. In fact, the same handful of positive and affirming supporters were being visited repeatedly, while those the pastor found less encouraging languished for pastoral care. Pastor Edwin fed his own self-concept as an effective agent of pastoral care through that small number of affirming parishioners.

Key 5: Understand the Interpersonal Communication Process

One of the most effective ways to improve interpersonal competence is to develop a more thorough understanding of the interpersonal communication process. "Interpersonal communication has a conscious body of knowledge that can be mastered and applied" (Griffin, 1987, p. 10). That body of knowledge is markedly different from the study of public, one-to-many communication. Concepts such as listening (Chapter 7), power in relationships (Chapter 9), conflict management (Chapter 10), forgiveness (Chapter 11), and personal persuasion (Chapter 12) are all a part of interpersonal communication. Pastors who are skilled at relationship building and inter-personal communication have mastered this body of material and are effective in its use.

Interpersonal communication builds upon a series of concepts that serve to best describe how the process works. These concepts, which combine to form the nucleus for a model of pastoral interpersonal communication, are presented in Chapter 2 in the development of an interpersonal communication model.

KEY CONCEPTS

The most time-consuming responsibilities of pastors involve interpersonal relationships. Yet laypeople often fail to recognize this enormous time commitment, and pastors feel less than qualified in interpersonal skills. But, dyadic communication can be learned. Keys to improving pastoral interpersonal communication include

- Develop new relationships
- Develop new interests
- Metacommunicate
- Increase self-awareness
- Understand the interpersonal communication process

MEANINGS MANIA

Word Bank

a. interpersonal communication
b. self-profile
c. metacommunication
d. self-concept
e. self-awareness

Definitions

_____ 1. Communication about communication
_____ 2. Communication between two people
_____ 3. The recognition of personal strengths and weaknesses
_____ 4. An instrument designed to assist a person in understanding himself or herself
_____ 5. A communicator's image of the self

UNLEASHING THE POWER
OF INTERPERSONAL COMMUNICATION

If you are currently a pastor, keep a log for one week of your minis-try. How much time do you spend in interpersonal activities? How does that compare with your public ministry time or your time alone? If you are not yet involved in pastoral ministry, ask a pastor for per-mission to shadow him or her in order to gather the same data.

Chapter 2

Models of Communication

A study of why people change from one medical doctor to another during times when they are healthy revealed that the change has little to do with technical competence in medicine. In fact, 85 percent of the time the change came because of poor "bedside manner" or other dysfunctions in interpersonal communication (Duncan and Clark, 1996).

Similarly, pastors often don't experience difficulties in a particular parish because of theological incompetence, ineffectiveness in organizational management, or lack of public speaking skills. Instead, many pastoral difficulties arise from a lack of bedside manner because of problems in interpersonal communication. As noted in Chapter 1, developing a clear understanding of the interpersonal communication process leads to greater competence in these dyadic relationships. This chapter focuses on developing such an understanding.

LINEAR MODEL

Training for public communication, or one-to-many communication as it is sometimes called, utilizes a linear model of communication. In the linear model, a speaker places a message on a channel. A listener receives that message. The listener may, or may not, choose to place a response on a similar channel. Either way, the focus is on the message or the channel. This model can be diagrammed as in Figure 2.1.

The linear model may adequately explain the nature of mass communication such as a sermon delivered over radio or television. The pastor who does such a broadcast may receive a listener response sometime during the week. The listener may choose the channel of e-

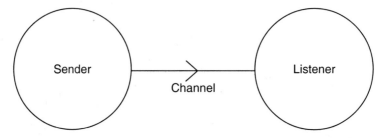

FIGURE 2.1. A Linear Model of Communication

mail or a phone call to carry his or her reaction to the broadcast message.

Difficulties arise when pastors behave as if interpersonal communication also functions according to the linear model. Notice the interpersonal communication dysfunction that develops in Pastoral Conversation 2.1 when Pastor Brook speaks in a hospital room as if interpersonal communication worked similar to her weekly broadcast.

Pastoral Conversation 2.1

Background

Pastor Brook has just stopped in at the hospital room of one of her parishioners, Ruby Jones. Unbeknownst to Pastor Brook, Ruby has just received some disturbing news from her physician about the nature of her illness and the prognosis.

Dialogue

PASTOR BROOK: Good morning, Ruby. How are you feeling today?

RUBY: Not so hot, really, Pastor.

PASTOR BROOK: I knew you would be better today. You even look better. It's God's involvement because of the prayer chain. Also the medicines are working by now. Medical science is a great gift God has given us, Ruby.

RUBY: I don't know. The doctor. . . . (She begins to cry.)

PASTOR BROOK: Of course it is a great gift from God, Ruby. Our God is a powerful God. Let's pray to that powerful God right now.

Analysis

1. How would you evaluate the effectiveness of Pastor Brook's hospital visit? In what ways was she less than effective? How could she have been more effective?
2. What one thing might Pastor Brook have done to improve her ministry to Ruby?

Clearly, Pastor Brook's interpersonal communication skills in this situation are weak. In Pastoral Conversation 2.1 she appears to communicate just as she would via the airwaves during her weekly radio broadcast. The emphasis is on Pastor Brook's intended message, while Ruby's words are virtually ignored. The linear model clearly does not adequately provide for Pastor Brook's current interpersonal communication scenario.

INTERACTIONAL MODEL

A second view of communication is sometimes referred to as interaction, the interactional model, or the interactive view (Stewart, 1973; Krivanek, 2000). This model moves a step closer to explaining interpersonal communication since it recognizes the involvement of more than one participant at the same time, and thus two-directional communication through what is sometimes called a feedback loop. The interactional model is diagrammed in Figure 2.2.

Pastors often find the interactional model adequate to explain preaching a Sunday morning sermon. In that setting an occasional nod of the head or raised eyebrow becomes the feedback that lets the pastor know the message either is, or is not, being understood. But usually the interactional model does not adequately explain the nature of interpersonal communication. In Pastoral Conversation 2.2, Pastor Brook interacts with Ruby along the lines of the interactional model. Notice how she acknowledges Ruby's feedback, but still fails to effectively communicate with her parishioner.

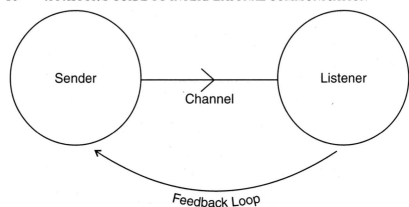

FIGURE 2.2. An Interactional Model of Communication

Pastoral Conversation 2.2

Background

The setting is the same as in Pastoral Conversation 2.1.

Dialogue

PASTOR BROOK: Good morning, Ruby. How are you feeling today?

RUBY: Not so hot, really, Pastor.

PASTOR BROOK: Still having those stomach pains, are you? Well, I've alerted the prayer chain and I'm sure the pain medications will also kick in very soon.

RUBY: It's not just that . . .

PASTOR BROOK: I know, Ruby. But, you can be sure that God hasn't forgotten your need. The Bible says, "God will never leave you nor forsake you." This is all going to come out just fine.

RUBY: I don't know, the doctor . . . (She begins to cry.)

PASTOR BROOK: There, there, Ruby; those stomach pains are really intense this morning, aren't they? Could I pray with you?

RUBY: (Unable to speak, simply shakes her head and closes her eyes.)

Analysis

1. Has Pastor Brook's communication improved when she acknowledges the feedback of Ruby? In what ways? In what ways has it not?
2. What one thing might Pastor Brook still do to improve her interpersonal communication with Ruby?

TRANSACTIONAL MODEL

Communication theorists often explain the process of interpersonal communication by means of the transactional model of communication (Berlo, 1960). The transactional model recognizes the simultaneous sending and receiving of messages, which more closely approximates a real life interpersonal communication scenario. It allows for the interaction of a receiver and a sender in a realistic information exchange. The model views interpersonal communication as a process rather than the product of a channel.

The transactional communication process can be likened to a business transaction such as a department store purchase. Here, both participants offer something to the relationship and both gain from the encounter. Simultaneous activities may occur, such as the clerk ringing up the transaction while the customer reaches for a purse or billfold. Pastor Brook becomes much more effective in her interaction with Ruby in Pastoral Conversation 2.3, when she communicates according to a transactional model.

Pastoral Conversation 2.3

Background

The situation is the same as in Pastoral Conversation 2.1.

Dialogue

PASTOR BROOK: Good morning, Ruby. How are you feeling today?
RUBY: Not so hot, really, Pastor.
PASTOR BROOK: Tell me about it, Ruby. Is it the stomach pains still?

RUBY: No. The doctor just came in to tell me I should have an operation to remove my gallbladder.

PASTOR BROOK: That's not what you wanted to hear, I'm sure.

RUBY: No, it sure wasn't. My mother died at a very early age from complications after gallbladder surgery. (She begins to cry.)

PASTOR BROOK: Ruby, I can tell you're upset. And, I can surely understand why. Yet, the advances God has allowed in medical science since your mother's death are remarkable. I feel confident you'll be as good as new in just a few days.

RUBY: That's what the doctor said, too.

PASTOR BROOK: Why don't we pray together for your doctor and for a successful surgery?

Analysis

1. In what ways has Pastor Brook improved in this dialogue over the first two attempts?
2. Was there one key moment in the dialogue in which Pastor Brook set the tone for a productive interpersonal exchange? What was it?

Some authors have attempted to diagram the transactional view of communication in a manner similar to the linear or interactional view (Adler and Towne, 2003; DeVito, 1998). The complexity of the process, however, makes such diagrams difficult to understand. Instead, transactional interpersonal communication is best understood through a series of rules.

PASTORAL INTERPERSONAL COMMUNICATION CONCEPTS

During times of war, military strategists develop what are known as rules of engagement. These rules define acceptable behavior for the soldier in the field, making clear under what circumstances it is appropriate to engage the enemy, and outlining appropriate actions within that engagement. While the rules of engagement vary from one conflict to another, or even between sectors within a conflict, anyone observing a participant's interaction with enemy combatants could soon determine the precise rules for the current campaign.

Similarly, in interpersonal communication "there are rules of the game to be deciphered by anyone who cares to watch" (Griffin, 1987, p. 18). The rules of pastoral interpersonal communication can be determined by careful observation. **P**astoral **I**nterpersonal **C**ommunication **C**oncepts (PICCs) are the pastor's rules of engagement. PICCs provide the best approach to understanding the transactional view of interpersonal communication, and they combine to support a transactional model of pastoral interpersonal communication.

PICC 1: Motivations Do Matter

A young female pastor tells of a third grade student in the Sunday school who brought her an apple nearly every Sunday. She assumed he was expressing appreciation and admiration for his pastor. In reality, the youth had a serious case of puppy love. Fortunately, the pastor realized his motivation in time to let the boy down gently. Until that time, however, there was little effective communication between the two, since every word spoken was seriously misinterpreted.

Another example of why motivations matter in interpersonal relationships occurred when Pastor Jon looked forward to an upcoming luncheon with the president of the seminary that was his alma mater. "Dr. Bigly will be in your area," the secretary had said, "and would like to take you to lunch in order to get better acquainted. He likes to stay in touch with prominent alums."

Pastor Jon felt honored and special that someone of Dr. Bigly's stature would take the time to meet with him. The phrase "prominent alums" replayed again and again in his mind. His ego rush slipped a bit, however, when Bigly revealed his true motivation for the luncheon. Bigly said, "I understand the wealthy industrialist Mr. Simpson is in your congregation. Would you introduce me so that I can challenge him to help the seminary financially?"

Had Pastor Jon anticipated Dr. Bigly's motives, that knowledge would have altered his anticipation as well as the nature of his initial conversation with the seminary president. Motivations make a profound difference, and understanding one another's motivations sets the stage for effective interpersonal communication.

People come to every interpersonal encounter with relational motivations. Notice how motivations matter in Pastoral Conversation 2.4,
where Pastor Dion assumes he is talking to a lighthearted and jovial
friend, when in fact he has a grieving parishioner on the phone.

Pastoral Conversation 2.4

Background

Pastor Dion is a member of the local service club in his community. Josh Bond, this year's club president, is a member of the congregation served by Pastor Dion. Frequently, Josh asks Pastor Dion to offer the invocation at the luncheon meeting. In fact, the two frequently
joke about Pastor Dion's role in the club as being only to pray. Pastor
Dion assumes when Josh calls on the telephone that his motivation is
the invocation for the club meeting next week.

Dialogue

PASTOR DION: (responding to the ringing telephone) Good morning,
   this is Pastor Dion.

JOSH: Pastor, this is Josh Bond.

PASTOR DION: Well, if it's not the president without a prayer.

JOSH: Actually, I did call for prayer. . . .

PASTOR DION: (interrupting) Why am I not surprised? Let me guess,
   you can't find anyone but the professionals to pray again this
   month.

JOSH: My mother died in the night, and . . .

Analysis

1. Is there anything Pastor Dion could have done to avoid this embarrassing situation?
2. What is Pastor Dion's best course of action now that he knows
   he has made a mistake?
3. What impact, if any, will mismatched motives likely have on the
   relationship between Josh and Pastor Dion in the future?

PICC 2: A Meeting of the Minds

When interpersonal communication is effective a meeting of the minds develops between participants. The more effective the communication becomes, the greater this overlap in thinking.

Pastor Stan was a student pastor in the Appalachian Mountains of eastern Kentucky. Previously, Stan had lived his entire twenty-three years of life in the flatlands of northwestern Ohio. Stan called at the home of one of the leaders of the church, Joel Dillar, during his first week of student ministry. On the front porch of the well-kept mountain cabin, Stan was surprised to hear Joel say, "Wouldn't care to have you come in, preacher." Since such phraseology to Stan meant that the homeowner was not interested in his coming in, Pastor Stan quickly backed off the porch and left. He assumed that he had interrupted something, or overstepped his bounds in some way. Where Stan came from such an expression meant he was not at all welcome at this time.

Only later did Stan discover that to the highlander the expression meant, "I have no cares at all about you coming in the house." It was in fact intended as a most cordial welcome. The meaning intended was just the opposite of that which Stan perceived.

Applying a series of diagrams to the conversation between Stan and his parishioner illustrates this rule. As shown in Figure 2.3, there was virtually no meeting of the minds. When Stan stepped onto the porch he had one understanding of the phrase, "Wouldn't care to have you come in." His parishioner had a much different understanding.

As time passed, Pastor Stan heard the expression, "Wouldn't care to have you come in," used repeatedly by members of his congregation, and other townsfolk as well. Within a few weeks Pastor Stan be-

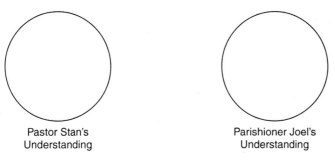

Pastor Stan's
Understanding

Parishioner Joel's
Understanding

FIGURE 2.3. Initial Interaction—No Meeting of the Minds

gan to develop a new awareness of the meaning of the phrase. He still did not totally understand what the local people meant, but he realized that there was a different meaning from the one he had grown up with. Figure 2.4 demonstrates the beginning of an overlap of understanding between Pastor Stan and Parishioner Joel. The two developed a meeting of the minds, even though they had no additional conversation about the matter.

About six weeks into the pastorate, Pastor Stan had a conversation with Parishioner Joel wherein he explained his quick exit during that first visit. The two jokingly compared other regional phrases after explaining what each meant by the expression, "Wouldn't care to have you come in." After the conversation, they had a nearly complete understanding of the phrase. Their meeting of the minds is illustrated in Figure 2.5.

Two people communicating interpersonally are limited by language and experience. As a result, they can never be certain that they have total agreement as to meaning. Thus, a small area is left without overlap even in the "mature understanding" diagram (Figure 2.5) of the encounter between Stan and Joel.

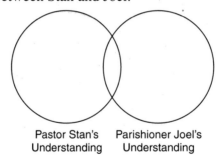

Pastor Stan's   Parishioner Joel's
Understanding   Understanding

FIGURE 2.4. Continuing Interaction—Developing Meeting of the Minds

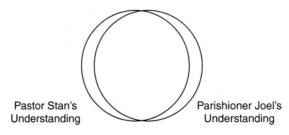

Pastor Stan's   Parishioner Joel's
Understanding   Understanding

FIGURE 2.5. Final Interaction—Nearly Complete Meeting of the Minds

The key to understanding the meeting of the minds concept lies in understanding that meaning is in minds, not in words or phrases. The meaning of the phrase, "Wouldn't care to have you come in," existed in the minds of the respective men, and not in the words themselves. For their communication to become effective the men had to come to a point of shared meaning concerning the key phrase.

Even though the meaning of words is not in the word itself, but in the minds of communicators, no particular problems arise if pastors use concrete terms. For example, the word "house" may mean a modest four-room bungalow to Pastor Aaron who lives in a small-town parsonage. The same word may imply a lavish estate mansion to Pastor Jason who grew up as the only child of wealthy parents, yet the men communicate with reasonable effectiveness because they share a basic understanding about the term used to indicate, "a building in which people live."

Problems may arise, however, when pastors begin to use the more abstract terms of theological language. The words "joy," "peace," "grace," and "love" may have vastly different meanings for two communicators.

As with abstract terms, theological concepts can create communication difficulties. One pastor seemed to make progress in an evangelistic call until he urged the woman of the house to "yield to the heavenly Father." She quickly excused herself and ran from the room, leaving her husband to explain to the baffled pastor that she had grown up in an abusive home where "yielding to father" constituted a dreadful way of life.

Sometimes the careful pastor must probe again and again for the meaning of a word or phrase that lies within another human being. That same pastor may also need to explain his or her own meaning in several different ways in order to establish clarity. The objective of achieving a meeting of the minds yields effective communication when thoroughly pursued, however.

PICC3: Inevitable, Irreversible, and Unrepeatable

Pastor Eric had just ten minutes until he was scheduled to be at an important finance committee meeting at the church. As he sat across the restaurant table from parishioner Matt Engels, he became increasingly anxious about the time. The two men had agreed to meet socially over lunch. It quickly became obvious, however, that Matt intended to use the time for an informal counseling session. For more than an hour he discussed his frustrations about raising teenagers. Abruptly though, the luncheon ended when Matt observed, "Obviously you're in a hurry, Pastor. I'd better let you go."

Nothing Pastor Eric could do or say at that point could convince Matt that his problem with a son was important enough to take a few extra minutes. Inadvertently, Pastor Eric had already communicated something quite different.

Pastor Eric said nothing verbally about the time, but Matt had gotten the unintended message from Pastor Eric's constant shifting, his glances at his watch, and his inattentive gaze. Any time two people are in proximity messages are being sent. Any behavior can communicate as long as another person is involved in the communication event and that person assigns a meaning to the message (Watzlawick, Beavin, and Jackson, 1967). "All behavior in an interactional setting communicates; therefore, if you are interacting with another person, all your behavior communicates something" (DeVito, 1998, p. 33).

Pastor Eric's experience in the restaurant with Matt also demonstrates another important element of PICC 3. That is, communication is irreversible. Children may demand of one another, "You take that back." In reality, however, taking back communiqués, whether intended or not, is an impossibility.

Communication is also unrepeatable, since it involves not just words and behaviors, but settings and a frame of reference as well. Pastor Lance was having a very difficult time with transition. He had accepted a call to a new parish, but was anxious about the first Sunday. A family member quipped with regard to Lance's anxiety, "Remember, you never get a second chance to make a first impression." Nor does one ever get a second chance at any other communication event. One can, of course, say, "Please, forget I said that"; or "I'm sorry"; or "Could we pretend that this evening never happened?" But, even if another agrees to new beginnings, the past remains.

PICC 4: Content As Well As Relationship

Every interpersonal communiqué includes both a content and relational aspect (Watzlawick, Beavin, and Jackson, 1967). Careful examination of the dialogue in Pastoral Conversation 2.5 helps to explain this rule of engagement.

Pastoral Conversation 2.5

Background

Pastor Tim is in his church office working on notes for the mid-week Bible study when the telephone rings.

Dialogue

PASTOR TIM: Hello. Pastor Tim speaking.
CALLER: This is Jan. You need to get over here right away.

This brief exchange cannot be effectively analyzed without knowing the identity of caller Jan and her relationship to Pastor Tim. For example, if Jan is Tim's spouse and Tim is fifty minutes late for dinner, Tim will respond on the basis of that relationship and scenario. On the other hand, what if Jan is the senior pastor of the church where Tim serves, and she is calling from the next office? In such a case this conversation may imply that Tim has made some grievous error, or that Jan has very little respect for her subordinates. If Jan is an elderly parishioner who has a serious heart problem and Tim has given her instructions to call him whenever she needs assistance, the analysis of the call is still different. Jan may be an overbearing church boss who has difficulty accepting Tim's authority and leadership. In this case the analysis, and thus Tim's response, will be still different.

In each scenario Pastor Tim will respond on the basis of the past relationship, not just to the current conversation, because he recognizes that every communication event has both relational and content aspects. He recognizes that the meaning of the same words is much different when those words are spoken by an angry spouse, a superior, a parishioner in need, or a disgruntled layperson. Relationship alters meaning.

By contrast, sometimes in a static relationship, content alters the meaning of a message. The elected layleader of a congregation may say to the pastor of her church, "Pastor, you are doing a great job of nursing home visitation." Or, she may say, "That was an excellent sermon on Sunday." In these two scenarios the content has changed. But, the fact that the layleader has some responsibility for pastoral oversight and evaluation remains the same. That is, the relationship is unchanged.

Research indicates that men focus more on the content of a communiqué, while women focus more on the relational aspects of a particular statement (Wood, 2005). Effective pastors of both genders, however, recognize that relationship and content are equally important parts of the message and its meaning. These effective pastors attempt to interpret and respond to both the relational and the content aspects of the message.

KEY CONCEPTS

The linear or interactional models of public address are much too simplistic for a proper understanding of pastoral interpersonal communication. For this more complex process, only the transactional model seems adequate. Four important PICCs are:

1. Motivations do matter
2. A meeting of the minds
3. Inevitable, irreversible, and unrepeatable
4. Content as well as relationship

These four form the basis of the transactional model of communication. The successful pastoral interpersonal communicator understands and effectively utilizes all four.

MEANINGS MANIA

Work Bank

    a. channel
    b. linear model
    c. feedback
    d. relational aspects of communication
    e. content aspects of communication
    f. message

g. interactional model
h. transactional model
i. sender
j. receiver
k. meeting of the minds

Definitions

_____ 1. A one-directional model of communication usually used to explain public address
_____ 2. One who receives a message
_____ 3. The common understanding that develops between two communicators
_____ 4. A bidirectional model of communication that allows for feedback
_____ 5. An aspect of a message that includes the words
_____ 6. An aspect of a message that includes the relationship between the communicators
_____ 7. The response of a receiver to a sender
_____ 8. Information conveyed from a sender to a receiver
_____ 9. One who transmits a message to another
_____ 10. The means by which a message is sent whether verbal, nonverbal, or written
_____ 11. The model that best explains interpersonal communication by relating it to a purchase

UNLEASHING THE POWER OF INTERPERSONAL COMMUNICATION

With permission, tape-record a conversation with a friend. Transcribe the tape into a written dialogue on the left column of a two-column format. In the right column note as many evidences of the four PICCs discussed in this chapter as you can find.

Chapter 3

Perception

Pastor Raphael avoided conversations with Dana Anderson whenever possible. "The woman is just so intense," he commented to his wife. "She makes me uncomfortable just listening to her, but since she is Sunday school superintendent, I have to work with her the best I can." That attitude did not prepare Pastor Raphael for the verbal barrage that Dana unleashed in his office the next Sunday morning just after the Sunday school hour. Their conversation appears in Pastoral Conversation 3.1.

Pastoral Conversation 3.1

Background

As Sunday school superintendent it was among Dana Anderson's responsibilities to arrange for substitutes when a teacher was absent. The task was made more difficult by the fact that occasionally teachers would not provide much warning of their intended absence. Angela Harmon, fifth grade teacher, had called just an hour before Sunday school to announce that her family had plans and she would not be teaching that morning. When Dana stepped into Pastor Raphael's office she was livid.

Dialogue

PASTOR RAPHAEL: Dana, what in the world has upset you so?

DANA: Angela Harmon, that's what. She called less than an hour before Sunday school to say she wasn't coming. She needed me to find a substitute. Apparently she thinks I've got nothing else to do but cater to her last-minute whims. The woman has no sense of responsibility, and no common courtesy. She's not good for our education program. I'm looking for her replacement. As soon as I find one, I intend to ask her to leave the Sunday school staff. And, I expect the full support of you as pastor.

PASTOR RAPHAEL: Please sit down a moment and try to relax. I'm sure your evaluation of Angela is accurate as you see it, but . . .

DANA: (interrupting, shouting) It's not the way I see it. That's the way it is!

Analysis

1. What is the most effective course of action for Pastor Raphael to take at this moment? What future actions will he need to take?
2. Is Dana's anger justified? Explain your answer.
3. Evaluate the statement, "That's not the way I see it. That's the way it is." How common is that attitude in today's culture? Why do you think so?

Dana Anderson has confused reality with her perceptions of reality with regard to both an individual and a situation. She believes that her perceptions of the problem are the same as the realities of that problem. Nor is she alone in modern culture. In fact, so prevalent is her viewpoint that the expression, "perception is reality" is commonly used to describe the power of perception.

Perception is powerful. It plays an especially powerful role in interpersonal relationships. But the idea that perception is the same as reality goes a bit too far. Moses discusses this very matter with God in Exodus, Chapter 3. God has announced from a burning bush that Moses is to be the leader of the people of Israel as they flee from bondage in Egypt. But Moses recognizes that it is one thing to perceive the call of God while listening to a dramatic voice speaking from a burning bush. It is quite another to recognize the voice of God as reported second-hand from a shepherd and would-be national leader. Moses puts the perception issue this way, "Suppose I go to the Israelites and say to them, 'The God of your fathers has sent me to you,' and they ask me, 'What is his name?' Then what shall I tell them?" (Exodus 3:13). Moses' concern is that the people's perception of God will be so vastly different from his own that they may not even be able to relate to his message. God's response serves to not only put Moses' mind at ease about his future leadership role, but also to clarify the relationship between perception and reality. God answers, "I AM WHO I AM" (Exodus 3:14).

This response demonstrates that God is not dependent upon the perceptions of people. God exists as an independent reality aside from anyone's perception. God, the independent reality, will not change on the basis of the perceptions of the people, or of Moses, or of any other human being.

A nineteenth-century poem by John Godfrey Saxe (1852) illustrates the same point by telling the story of six blind men.

The Perception of Six Blind Men

It was six men of Indostan
To learning much inclined
Who went to see an elephant
Though all of them were blind,
That each by observation
Might satisfy his mind.

The first approached the elephant,
And happening to fall
Against the broad and sturdy side,
At once began to bawl;
"Why bless me, but the elephant
Is very much like a wall."

The second, feeling the tusk
Cried, "Ho, What have we here?
So very round and smooth and sharp,
To me 'tis very clear
This wonder of an elephant
Is very much like a spear."

The third approached the animal
And, happening to take
The squirming trunk within his hands
Thus boldly he spake:
"I see," quoth he, "the elephant
Is very much like a snake."

The fourth reached out his eager hand
And felt about the knee

"What most this wondrous beast is like
Tis very plain," quoth he
"Tis clear enough the elephant
Is very much like a tree!"

The fifth, who chanced to touch the ear,
Said, "Even the blindest man
Can tell what this resembles most,
Deny the fact who can
This marvel of an elephant
Is very much like a fan!"

The sixth no sooner had begun
About the beast to grope
Then seizing on the swinging tail
That fell within his scope
"I see," quoth he, "the elephant
Is very much like a rope."

And so these men of Indostan
Disputed loud and long,
Each in his own opinion
Exceedingly stiff and strong.
Though each was partly right,
They all were very wrong.

Notice that the perceptions of the blind men did not change that reality known as an elephant. Yet, as with Dana Anderson, they all
shouted concerning the beast, "That's not the way I see it. That's the
way it is!"

THE PERCEPTION PROCESS

One reason that perception is sometimes confused with reality is
that perception is the only means a communicator has of observing
reality. Perception is the process a communicator uses to become
aware of the world. "Interpersonal perception concerns the way we
sense, organize, and interpret-evaluate information about people"
(DeVito, 1990, p. 82).

The perception process can be illustrated by means of a funnel as shown in Figure 3.1.

The Ss grouped around the funnel mouth represent perceptual stimuli in various forms. The words of a colleague, the persuasive message of an advertiser, the touch of a friend, all join with thousands of other stimuli vying for the attention of a given communicator.

Only certain stimuli ever reach the consciousness of a communicator, however. An individual's perceptual filters effectively select the others out. These filters may be conscious as in turning off the radio when a certain program comes on or a particular song is played. Such perceptual filters may also come into play when a pastor discounts the words of the town gossip or avoids a parishioner who tends to be constantly negative.

Perceptual filters may be subconscious. These filters may have developed over long years of personal experience with certain personality types or professional groups. Whether conscious or subconscious, the perceptual filters eliminate many stimuli and allow select others deeper into the perceptual funnel. Here the stimuli are organized according to a pattern that has meaning for the communicator. Figure 3.2 illustrates this organizing process.

How many cubes a perceiver sees depends upon whether the dark surface is the top of a cube or the bottom. Are there ten or twelve

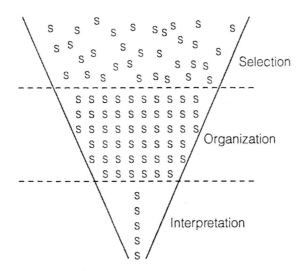

FIGURE 3.1. The Perception Process

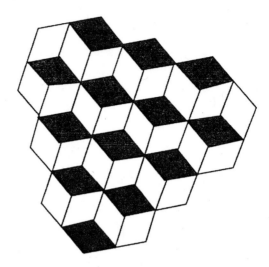

FIGURE 3.2. How Many Stacked Cubes? (Artwork by Tracy Thurman.)

stacked cubes? One student who examined the drawing quickly concluded that there were twenty-two. Indeed, the dark surface could be on both the top and the bottom of cubes. Most communicators fail to see the big picture of reality. Instead they mentally declare, "That's not the way I see it. That's the way it is. There are ten (or twelve)!"

Communicators organize their views of other communicators in much the same way they organize their view of objects such as the cubes. The organizational system a communicator uses is made up of perceptual schema. Perceptual schema may cause an individual to be classified on the basis of appearance, traits, or memberships. Sometimes the perceptual schema of an individual organizes people according to their professional roles.

One pastor noted that she was less effective at evangelism than some of her key laypeople. The reason, she believed, was that when laypeople declared that their faith made a difference in their lives, people listened. They expected pastors to hold to that view, however. In effect she observed that unchurched community members tended to organize evangelistic appeals along the perceptual schema of professional roles.

Once perceptions have been selected and organized they must be interpreted in a way that makes sense to the perceiver. A communicator who views an object or another human being subconsciously applies a series of guidelines to the perceptual interpretation. These interpretive guidelines help determine whether the perceptual event will be seen positively or negatively.

INTERPRETIVE GUIDELINES

Relational Satisfaction

Research demonstrates that when a communicator is happy with a partner there is a tendency to positively interpret that partner's behaviors (Bradbury and Fincham, 1990). The converse is also true. Thus the status of a relationship has much to do with the interpretation of current events within that relationship. Often two people in a relationship develop what communication scholars refer to as shared perception or narrative (Griffin, 2003). For example, several coworkers in the same office may come to perceive "differential treatment" by management toward one of their number in similar ways (Sias, 1996). These shared narratives are not necessarily accurate, but they are nonetheless powerful.

Most churches have a shared narrative that they are a friendly and open congregation. However, those trying to break in from the outside may develop a much different interpretation. The shared narrative has less to do with how the church behaves toward others than how its members feel about one another and their life together.

Expectations

Whenever a communicator expects another to act in a certain way, those expectations are quite frequently realized. In fact, the expectation itself often leads to the reality. Social science researchers refer to this phenomenon as self-fulfilling prophecy (Insel and Jacobson, 1975). The self-fulfilling prophecy generally follows a series of predictable steps.

1. One communicator makes a prediction about another communicator. (A parishioner believes that Pastor Paul is not very skilled in home visitation.)
2. The predictor acts toward the other as if the prediction were fact. (When Pastor Paul visits, the parishioner behaves as if he lacked interpersonal skill in the situation.)
3. Action creates reality. (Pastor Paul becomes tense and awkward as a result of his treatment.)
4. Beliefs are reinforced. (The parishioner observes Pastor Paul's lack of effectiveness in home visitation and the prophetic attitude is intensified.)

Self-Concept

A communicator's self-concept has a great deal of impact on how he or she interprets a situation or the behavior of another. One team of researchers discovered that self-concept was a key factor in interpreting whether someone was teasing or being hostile (Alberts and Kellar-Guenther, 1996). And, in another study it was observed that the loneliness of a perceiver had tremendous impact on the interpretation of a received message (Edwards and Bello, 2001).

Whether one's self-concept includes happy or sad, competent or incompetent, fearful or confident, it will alter the interpretation of the messages of others. In general, a person with high self-esteem is more likely to have a high opinion of others, while a person with low self-esteem has a lower opinion of others (Baron, 1974).

Circumstances

The circumstances under which a message comes to a receiver plays a major role in determining how that message is interpreted. For example, the persuasive impact of a billboard advertisement for fast food is interpreted more favorably just before meal time than it is on a full stomach. Similarly, in Pastoral Conversation 3.1, if Pastor Raphael were to realize that Dana had been downsized out of her job during the past week he may respond much differently to her attitude toward Angela Harmon than if his knowledge of the situation includes that Dana has a reputation for inappropriate aggressiveness.

The fact that circumstances surrounding a communicator's behavior alter the interpretation of that behavior make it essential to explore, as much as possible, the context of an interpersonal communiqué. Effective pastoral perceivers ask relevant questions, listen carefully to responses, and observe both verbal and nonverbal messages all in an attempt to gain an appreciation for the circumstances surrounding a message.

Timing

The fifth interpretive guideline, timing, is closely related to circumstances. Here the issue is not so much what else is going on in a communicator's life or the situation surrounding his or her message, as when it is that the perception comes to the interpreter.

For example, is the message part of a first impression? First impressions are inevitable, but often inaccurate. They may be based more on appearance or attire than on deeper criteria. DeVito (1990) notes that, "We see the injustice of first impressions most clearly with shy people. Frequently these individuals seem unfriendly. If we form a first impression of unfriendliness, we may never get a chance to see the real friendly but shy person underneath" (p. 92).

But the issue of timing of perceptions is not solely about first impressions. One social science pioneer (Asch, 1946) noted the impact of not only the first message interpreted, but also the most recent. His study used a list of adjectives to describe a person. Perceptions of the person were most significantly influenced by the first and last adjectives on the list. His research demonstrated that what comes first, the primacy effect, has great power on interpretation. But, so too does what comes last, the recency effect. Clearly the timing of a message has a great deal to do with the receiver's perceptual interpretation.

Consistency

Communicators may maintain internal consistency. Thus an important guideline used in interpreting certain stimuli comes from answering the question, "What is the most consistent way to interpret this new information?"

Pastor Kevin repeatedly observed bruises on one of the little boys who came without his family to the Sunday school. He asked the youngster about the bruises and was told, "I think I fall down a lot." Notice how Pastor Kevin will likely draw his conclusion about the matter on the basis of consistency with other information. What will Pastor Kevin conclude if each of the following circumstances is also true?

- The boy's father is a well-respected businessman and his mother an active social service volunteer in the community.
- The little boy comes from a single-parent welfare family.
- The boy's father has recently been accused of battery in a domestic dispute with a live-in girlfriend.
- Pastor Kevin grew up in an abusive home.
- Pastor Kevin's own son is frequently falling and bruising himself.

Pastor Kevin will interpret the new stimuli on the basis of consistency with what has already been perceived. A more thorough view of consistency and its role in balance theories is presented in Chapter 11.

PERCEPTUAL SHORTCUTS

This chapter has thus far explored how certain stimuli are processed through the perceptual funnel and how the process leads the communicator to a new perspective on reality. Often, however, the process of observation, selection, and interpretation is short-circuited. Perceptual shortcuts can lead to a distorted view of reality. Effective pastoral communicators will want to carefully avoid three very common perceptual shortcuts: stereotyping, implying characteristics, and attribution error.

Stereotyping

In the earliest days of printing, typesetting was a long and laborious process. Later a plate was molded whereby multiple copies could be produced from one act of typesetting. These plates became known as stereotypes. Today the word stereotype refers to the process of shortcutting perceptions of individual people by lumping together all people within a certain group and assuming they all possess the same characteristics. Such stereotyping usually follows a prescribed three-step pattern.

1. A perceiver categorizes people on the basis of an easily identified characteristic. Gender or race is thought to be the most common.
2. The perceiver attributes a set of characteristics to most or all members of that group. For example:
     Most men are _____.
     Women typically _____.
     Hispanics usually _____.
     Most African Americans _____.
     Anglos generally _____.
3. The perceiver applies the set of characteristics to an individual because he or she is a member of the group. For example, since Kelly is a woman she is expected to nag. Since Leonard is a white male he is expected to be aggressive.

A person can quickly measure his or her own tendency to stereotype by considering reactions to members of certain groups such as the following:

Asians	Teenagers
Women in ministry	Democrats
Hispanics	Republicans
Stay-at-home parents	Baptists
Senior adults	Episcopalians

Everyone has attitudes about these and other groups. This is not wrong. The shortcut develops when a communicator labels an individual without getting to know him or her personally. That is, without using the perceptual process to formulate intelligent reactions to stimuli.

Although it is common to identify stereotyping of those of another race or gender, other types of stereotyping also exist. Pastors must also avoid the communication problems that can develop as a result of stereotyping those of a certain age group. All teens are not alike. All senior adults do not behave the same way.

Implying Characteristics

A second shortcut to the perceptual process is implying characteristics. Implying characteristics can best be understood in light of a theory known as implicit personality theory. According to the theory, every individual has an implied system of internal rules that determine which characteristics of an individual go with which other characteristics (Cohen, 1983). For example, an individual may have a very positive set of experiences with Christians, and so implicitly attributes many positive characteristics to all Christians. Implying characteristics may go well beyond items associated with the faith. To determine that Christians attend church on Sunday morning may be one thing, but it is quite another to conclude that all Christians are always happy, or never consume an adult beverage, or practice impeccable integrity.

Implying characteristics may lead a perceiver to see positive qualities in a person when in fact those qualities do not exist. One pastor reported seeing glowing characteristics in a particular elderly member of his congregation. The lady in question reminded him of his grandmother. He applied to the parishioner all of the qualities he recalled in that grandmother. Many of those qualities simply did not exist in the parishioner.

Implying characteristics may cause a communicator to overlook or distort certain negative qualities because they do not conform to the personality assigned to that individual. Martha Secor lavishly complimented Pastor Cathleen on her Sunday morning sermons. As a result, Pastor Cathleen believed Martha to be a person of good judgment, positive outlook, and friendliness. Pastor Cathleen failed to see Martha as manipulative and aggressively seeking power. In fact, most of the people in the congregation recognized these more negative qualities in Martha's personality.

Attribution Error

A third shortcut to the perception process is based upon attribution theory. According to the theory, a communicator spends a great deal of time and energy trying to discover why people do what they do (Jones and Davis, 1965). That is attempting to attribute motives to behaviors. Attribution itself is not necessarily wrong. In fact, accurate attribution is an important part of understanding others. Attribution can lead to concluding that people's behavior is determined more by internal factors than by external circumstances.

Pastor Christopher noted that Michelle was frequently late for committee meetings at the church. He attributed her tardiness to irresponsibility. In reality, Michelle found it difficult to arrive at the church by seven o'clock since her husband frequently did not arrive home from work until just a few minutes before seven. At that point they quickly passed off responsibility for the couple's two-year-old child. Pastor Christopher short-circuited the perceptual process by means of an attribution error.

One common attribution error arises from attributing everything in a person's repertoire of behaviors to a single circumstance. As a result of limited counseling skills and exposure to a great deal of confidential personal history, pastors may be particularly susceptible to this error, sometimes called overattribution.

Pastor Sean knew that Hugh had experienced a particularly difficult childhood. Hugh was put up for adoption in elementary school because his parents simply could not afford to feed their six children. As a result Pastor Sean tended to dismiss all of Hugh's attitudinal problems by attributing them to that one major childhood trauma. One has to admire Pastor Sean's sensitivity to Hugh's experience. Yet viewing everything Hugh said or did in light of one incident in his background was neither an accurate view of reality nor helpful to Hugh.

KEY CONCEPTS

Perception is not reality, but it is extremely powerful in interpersonal communication. Pastoral communicators should examine personal perceptions. Quality perceptions grow out of the process of selecting, organizing, and interpreting stimuli. Guidelines for interpreting stimuli in the formation of perceptions include

- Relational satisfaction
- Expectations
- Self-concept
- Circumstances
- Timing
- Consistency

Perceptions are much more likely to be an accurate reflection of reality when the pastoral perceiver avoids stereotyping, implying characteristics, or attributing.

MEANINGS MANIA

Word Bank

a. perception
b. perceptual schema
c. stereotyping
d. perception process
e. self-fulfilling prophecy
f. implicit personality theory
g. perceptual filters
h. interpretative guidelines
i. attribution theory

Definitions

_____ 1. A theory that says communicators search for the reasons for others' behaviors

_____ 2. An individual's view of reality

_____ 3. Believing a certain thing about a person or event helps cause that thing to happen

_____ 4. Believing that all people in a certain group have identical characteristics

_____ 5. Either consciously or subconsciously ignoring certain stimuli

_____ 6. The process statements by which a communicator makes sense of certain stimuli

_____ 7. The patterns by which stimuli are organized within a communicator

_____ 8. The selecting, organizing, and interpreting of stimuli

_____ 9. Every person has an internal framework of rules that declare which characteristics in an individual go with other characteristics

UNLEASHING THE POWER
OF INTERPERSONAL COMMUNICATION

Observe a stranger in a public place such as a fast-food restaurant or the student center. What are your perceptions of the individual? How would those perceptions change if you were aware that the person was on the way to a parent's funeral? How about if you knew that he or she worked as a secret service agent? Would your perceptions be different if you knew the person was running from an abusive spouse? What do these changes indicate about your use of the perception process? Do you stereotype? Do you imply characteristics? Do you tend toward the attribution error?

Chapter 4

Self-Disclosure

Two little boys were overheard visiting during the Sunday school hour at their local church. "I'm worried about my grandma," one of the boys said with a long sad face.

"Why?" his friend asked. "Is your grandma sick or something?"

"I'm not sure. I guess not really sick. She talks to herself."

The pair sat quietly for a few moments considering the gravity of the revelation. Finally the would-be helper offered this insight. "I don't think it's anything to worry about. After all, Pastor Randy talks to himself every Sunday. He thinks the whole congregation is listening."

Hopefully Pastor Randy has a few listeners to the morning message. In fact, what may be a greater issue for Pastor Randy than talking *to* himself is talking *about* himself. As with many pastors, Randy may be questioning how much of what the experts call self-disclosure is appropriate for pastoral relationships.

SELF-DISCLOSURE DEFINED

Adler and Towne (2003) define self-disclosure as "the process of deliberately revealing information about oneself that is significant and that would not normally be known by others" (p. 337). Johnson (1997) offers a definition that is a bit more precise with regard to the content of the disclosure. He believes that self-disclosure involves revealing how a person is reacting to the present situation. In addition, he notes that the process involves giving information about the past that is relevant to an understanding of those reactions.

Regardless of the exact definition, to be labeled self-disclosure a communiqué must meet three important criteria according to Cozby (1973, p. 75). These are:

1. It must contain personal information about the self.
2. The sender must communicate the information verbally.
3. Another person must be the intentional target.

Self-disclosing communication may be considered in terms of breadth and depth of topic. Two pastors who meet for the first time at their denomination's annual meeting may discuss a host of topics ranging from the weather, to their favorite sport's team, to family, to the demographics of their local church. The pair is likely to engage in conversation on a wide breadth of topics, but have very little self-disclosing depth in the discussion. Such depth comes when a dyadic pair reveals greater insights about a particular topic to one another.

In contrast to the two pastors who meet at the annual meeting, two pastors from neighboring communities who are lifelong friends are more likely to use their conversation time to discuss particular issues in-depth, rather than exploring a breadth of topics. Powell (1969) identifies the following five levels of communication. Conversational dyads, which move down the list, are engaging in ever-increasing depth of discussion.

Level 1: Cliché. Cliché conversation includes phrases such as, "Hi. How are you?" Most pastors engage in such superficial phrases scores of times each day. An expanded lexicon of twenty-first-century clichés includes the popular, "Have a nice day," spoken to strangers by senders who have no interest at all in the outcome of the receiver's day.

Level 2: Facts. Facts represent an only slightly deeper level of communiqué. In the communication of facts there is no opportunity for disagreement or debate. As a result, most dyads view facts as "safe talk."

Level 3: Opinions. The ideas and judgments of the sender are included in this level of communication. These opinions may or may not be shared by a receiver, thus some risk is involved in this level of communication. Further, since opinions can be held in silence and never discovered by another, clearly this level of communication involves the beginning of genuine self-disclosure.

Level 4: Emotions. Feelings about a circumstance, event, or relationship comprise the fourth level of communication. The disclosure of emotion puts a sender at great risk of misunderstanding and the relationship at risk of destruction. As a result, this level of self-disclosure is usually reserved for only the best ongoing relationships. The greatest relational rewards await those who are willing to reveal their innerselves at the emotional level.

Level 5: Peak communication. Peak communication involves an open sharing of innermost secrets. This is seldom achieved and always reserved for the most intimate relationships.

HOW SELF-DISCLOSURE WORKS

Joseph Luft and Harrington Ingham combined their own first names to identify their Johari window (Luft, 1969). The Johari window is a four-pane window formed by the intersection of information an individual knows about the self with the information known by the other person in the relationship. The resultant window provides a general overview of the nature of self-disclosure. Figure 4.1 illus-

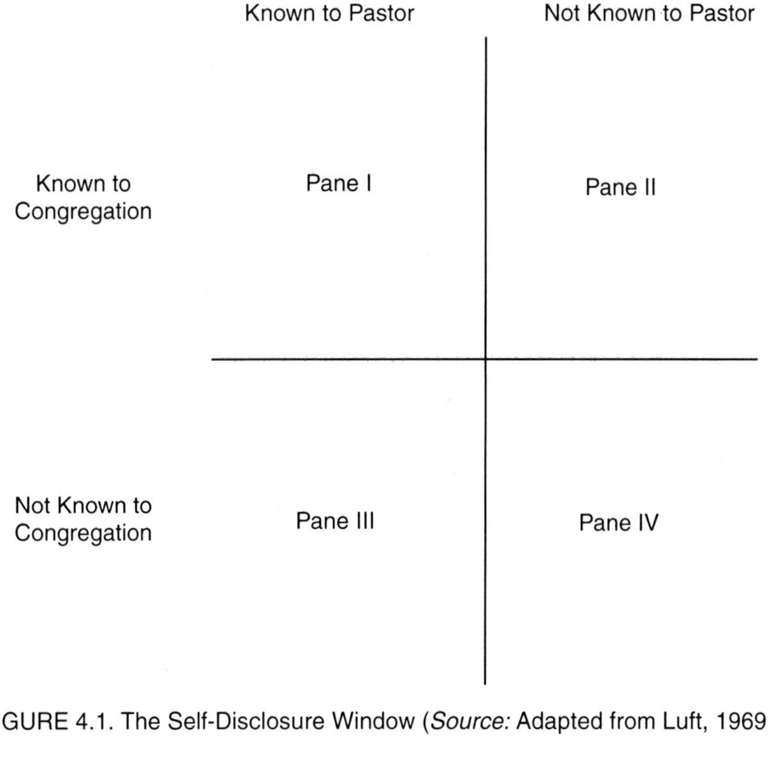

	Known to Pastor	Not Known to Pastor
Known to Congregation	Pane I	Pane II
Not Known to Congregation	Pane III	Pane IV

FIGURE 4.1. The Self-Disclosure Window (*Source:* Adapted from Luft, 1969.)

trates the creation of the four panes as they might appear in the context of a pastor and congregation.

Pane I, the open pane, contains all the information realized by the pastor and also recognized by the people in the congregation. No secrets lie in the open pane. Pastor Irwin hates making hospital calls and makes no attempt to hide that fact. The information is in pane I for all the members of his congregation.

Pane II, the blind pane, represents all those areas recognized by members of the congregation, but not recognized by the pastor. A pastor who had been converted and called to ministry from a background in a poverty-stricken home was called to an upper-middle-class suburban church. Some in the congregation recognized symptoms of his low self-image as he struggled with his own identity. He, however, was blind to those image issues and thus could not disclose about them.

Pane III, the hidden pane, is composed of elements of a pastor's life that are self-recognized but hidden from others. A pastor who had battled a serious problem with the use of pornography prior to his conversion decided his ministry was best served by not revealing that fact to anyone in the congregation. All experiences, emotions, and attitudes about pornography remained in the hidden pane.

Pane IV is called the unknown pane. Information in this pane is not recognized by anyone involved in the relationship. Pastor Dennis grew up on the mission field. He had no conscious realization of the impact that boarding school had on his formative years. Others with whom he had developed interpersonal relationships failed to recognize that impact as well for many years. Ultimately, a professional counselor assisted Dennis in uncovering some deep fears and inhibitions growing out of the boarding school experience.

The four panes in the self-disclosure window are interdependent. As one pane grows through self-realization and/or self-disclosure, another necessarily shrinks. Further, the window is unique to each individual relationship and even to particular topics within a given relationship.

For example, Pastor Jerry's personal views on stewardship have been fully discussed with Gloria, chairperson of the Finance Committee at Calvary Church. Jerry has never discussed stewardship with Cecil, the trustee, however. Figure 4.2 demonstrates the two windows

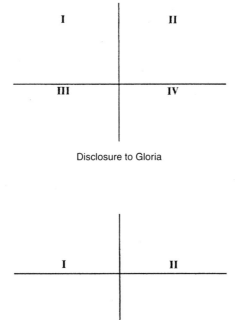

Disclosure to Gloria

Disclosure to Cecil

FIGURE 4.2. Pastor Jerry's Disclosure on Stewardship

representing Pastor Jerry's self-disclosure on stewardship to Gloria and Cecil.

WHY DO PASTORS SELF-DISCLOSE?

Some of the reasons that people self-disclose are appropriate and relationship-enhancing. Other reasons are more likely to damage on-going relationships because of their inappropriateness. Derlega and Grzelak (1979) suggest five reasons why people self-disclose.

- Catharsis
- Self-validation
- Self-clarification

- Reciprocity
- Relationship enhancement

Catharsis

Some self-disclosure is more a matter of "getting it off one's chest" than it is about real relationship building or intimacy. Hill and O'Brien (1999) address the issue of self-disclosure in therapeutic settings. Their observation bears general truth, however, when they write, "Finally, helpers sometimes inappropriately use self-disclosure to satisfy their own need—to relieve anxiety . . ." (p. 223). Such may be the case of the self-disclosure by Pastor Barry in Pastoral Conversation 4.1.

Pastoral Conversation 4.1

Background

Pastor Barry has grown increasingly frustrated with the low summer attendance at Trinity Church as the people travel for vacations and reunions. On a Monday morning, Pastor Barry is seated alone in the local coffee shop. Howard Martin, a key layperson from Trinity, has just walked in.

Dialogue

HOWARD: Good morning, Pastor. May I join you?

PASTOR BARRY: Please do. I would welcome the company.

HOWARD: How did the services go yesterday? I took my father to our family reunion up north. You remember Dad. At his age we think that every reunion might be his last.

PASTOR BARRY: We missed you, along with about thirty others. I don't know what to do about the summer attendance problem.

HOWARD: Don't get too discouraged, Pastor. You're doing a great job. It's just that a lot of people have things going on during the summer. Church attendance will pick up again in the fall. You'll see.

PASTOR BARRY: I'm not much on living in the future. The present realities are that Trinity is a part-time church. I'm called to be a full-time pastor. I'm not sure what I'll be doing come fall.

HOWARD: Pastor, this sounds serious. I hope you are not thinking of leaving Trinity. A lot of us would be very sorry to loose you as our pastor.

PASTOR BARRY: Obviously not sorry enough to commit to Trinity Church.

Analysis

1. Are Pastor Barry's feelings justified? Is his self-disclosure of those feelings appropriate? How are these two questions the same? How are they different?
2. How would you answer question 1 differently if Howard was:
    The chairman of the board at Trinity?
    A fellow pastor from another congregation?
    An unchurched member of the community?
    One who attends Trinity 50 of 52 Sundays?
    One who attends Trinity 5 of 52 Sundays?

Pastor Barry may have allowed his mood to interfere with interpersonal judgment. He may, upon later reflection, wish he had not said quite so much about his attitude toward Trinity's summer attendance. Self-disclosure should not be viewed as an excuse to say whatever is on one's mind. Greenberg, Rice, and Elliott (1993) label such cathartic self-disclosure as promiscuous self-disclosure, noting that in the case of a client-therapist relationship it may lead to a lessening of respect by the client for the therapist. A similar outcome could plague the pastor-parishioner relationship as well.

Self-Validation

Pastors may self-disclose for self-validation. Self-validation may also be at work in Pastoral Conversation 4.1. Self-validation includes all those disclosures that are made in order to enhance the disclosing pastor's image before the other person in the dyad, or to validate the opinions and attitudes of the one disclosing.

Pastor Barry may be attempting to communicate to Howard that his pain about the attendance problem is real. Perhaps he even hopes that Howard will act as a gatekeeper of the information, and let others in the congregation know it is important to become more regular in attendance. Although an attempt at social control raises serious issues about integrity and ethics, it is not an altogether uncommon use of pastoral self-disclosure.

One case of using self-disclosure as a means of self-validation involved Pastor Wendy. Parishioners noted that Pastor Wendy spent an unusual amount of interpersonal conversation time talking about her previous pastoral experiences. Sometimes it seemed she even violated ethics as she revealed situations and how she dealt with them in previous pastorates. In reality, as a woman in ministry, Pastor Wendy felt the need to be sure that everyone in the congregation was aware of her pastoral experience. She was using self-disclosure as a way to project a desired image.

Pastor Randall followed a colleague who had been dismissed by the congregation for marital infidelity. Pastor Randall often disclosed his affection for his wife, Paula, to people in the church and in public settings. He reasoned that such self-disclosure helped the congregation regain stability and build confidence in their new spiritual leader. Pastor Randall was thus using self-disclosure as self-validation.

Although self-validation is a common use of pastoral self-disclosure, the wise pastor will be very certain that motivations for self-disclosure are ethical. The ethics of self-disclosure typically means being open and honest about the reasons for the disclosure. Hidden agendas are usually not ethical.

Self-Clarification

A third reason for pastoral self-disclosure, self-clarification, also raises ethical concerns. This self-disclosure occurs when a pastor reveals an attitude, position, or emotion in order to internally confirm a belief or validate a behavior.

Suppose that after the exchange between Pastor Barry and Howard in Pastoral Conversation 4.1, Barry realized that he had said more than was appropriate. He self-clarifies by responding to Frank, "Howard's casual attitude about missing last Sunday just pushed me to say too much." Barry is now attempting to justify or clarify himself. He is using self-disclosure in order to clarify previous behaviors.

Pastor Tom was engaged in a counseling situation when he remarked, "I really don't see myself as a counselor, but since you've asked, here's what I think." He has self-disclosed in an attempt to clarify his perceived lack of counseling skills, but Tom's approach will likely not be very helpful to the counselee.

Hill and O'Brien (1999) believe that in many therapeutic situations the overwhelming responsibilities of the helper lead to self-clarification. They write, "Sometimes helpers disclose because their own problems are so overwhelming that they cannot attend to the client" (p. 223). With similar caution Pearson (2003) advises nurses to use self-clarification carefully. Her words apply to pastoral caregivers as well. "If disclosing our personal problems meets our own need, then we're hardly helping the patient" (p. 4).

Reciprocity

Another reason for pastors to self-disclose is reciprocity. Self-disclosure by one party in a dyad leads to an increased likelihood of self-disclosure by another. This truth is used by people helpers in general and pastors in particular to assist others. Pastor Wayne attempts to use self-disclosure to assist Caleb in responding to a call to ministry in Pastoral Conversation 4.2.

Pastoral Conversation 4.2

Background

Caleb is a high school student who is very active in the church that Pastor Wayne leads. Caleb has asked for a moment to talk with Pastor Wayne, but is obviously very nervous and unable to say what is really on his mind.

Dialogue

CALEB: So I . . . Well, what I wanted . . . I wonder how did you know. . . ?

PASTOR WAYNE: Caleb, you seem pretty upset about something.

CALEB: Yeah. Well I was wondering . . . ? Maybe I better come back another time.

PASTOR WAYNE: You know, Caleb, you remind me a lot of myself a few years ago.

CALEB: Really? How?

PASTOR WAYNE: When I first experienced a call to ministry, the idea made me so nervous I couldn't even say it out loud.

CALEB: Wow! How did you get over it?

PASTOR WAYNE: It seemed as if once I just said it out loud that first time, things changed. After that, it was much easier to seek advice and follow God's plan.

CALEB: You're right, Pastor. I've been wondering about a call. How did you know if God had called you to ministry and what did you do first to prepare?

Analysis

1. In what ways did self-disclosure reciprocity help Pastor Wayne in his effort to help Caleb?
2. What are the dangers in the approach? How can those risks be overcome?

Relationship Enhancement

Communication researchers agree that appropriate self-disclosure can serve to enhance an ongoing and healthy relationship. The key is for the disclosure to be appropriate. But determining what is meant by appropriate self-disclosure may not always be easy. Several factors combine to create an environment of appropriate self-disclosure.

One factor that makes self-disclosure an appropriate relationship enhancer is that in an initial encounter it is best not to disclose negatives (Blau, 1964). Vanleer (1987) concurs, suggesting that such information can damage a relationship if revealed too early.

In addition to the importance of self-disclosure occurring in an ongoing relationship, there must be a high level of trust between the two members of a disclosing dyad. Healey (1990) lists trust along with relationship as the two conditions that make self-disclosure appropriate. As trust develops in a relationship, the stage is set for deeper and deeper disclosures. As a result, most observers recognize that self-disclosure occurs incrementally. Self-disclosure that dumps everything needing to be said in one marathon session is not a relationship builder.

Gilbert (1976) demonstrated that self-disclosure is best done in moderation. She believes the highest level of satisfaction for both dyadic participants comes from a moderate level of disclosure while both low- and high-level disclosure lead to reduced relational satisfaction.

Finally, Hahn (2001) points out that self-disclosure is most effective in relationship enhancement when it is authentic as opposed to transparent. Authentic self-disclosure reveals the real person, including some inhibitions or unexplored areas. Transparency, on the other hand, reveals everything. Hahn suggests that transparency makes a self-discloser appear to be clothed in Saran Wrap. Obviously such disclosure may make an interpersonal partner uneasy and counteract any intended relational enhancement.

Combining these factors forces the pastoral self-discloser to conclude that self-disclosure will enhance a relationship when it is

- Part of an ongoing relationship
- Part of a trusting relationship
- Incremental
- Moderate
- Authentic

WHY DON'T PASTORS SELF-DISCLOSE?

Given the several positive advantages of self-disclosure, one might reasonably ask why pastors aren't more likely to self-disclose. The answer is that self-disclosure carries some risks. A pastor may simply not be willing to take the chances necessary to gain the benefits of self-disclosure.

Rosenfield (1979) discovered that males and females avoid self-disclosure for different reasons. Male pastors probably do not disclose to avoid loosing control of a relationship or to avoid appearing inconsistent to the other. Female pastors, on the other hand, probably avoid self-disclosure out of fear that the information will be used against them. In addition, they may feel that self-disclosure is a sign of emotional distress or that it might damage the relationship in the long run.

Some reasons pastors don't self-disclose more than they do can apply to both genders. Jourard (1971) notes that both males and females have two simple reasons to avoid self-disclosure. First, they assume no one is interested. Second, they honestly do not know how to comfortably go about self-disclosure.

Confession is good for the soul. One pastor noted, "It may be good for the soul, but it's hard on the reputation." Such a quip points to arguably the single most significant reason that pastors fail to self-disclose—a lowering of professional status. Pastors often feel that as spiritual leaders they must hide their true selves, since self-disclosure may involve admitting weakness, perhaps even sin. Such disclosures do carry the risk of lowered pastoral image and effectiveness among parishioners, and in some cases pastoral self-disclosure can lead to serious reactions on the part of parishioners.

Pastor Alonzo believed he was acting responsibly and above reproach when he disclosed his personal feelings about the church secretary to Larry, the chairperson of the church's personnel committee. Pastor Alonzo admitted that he gained emotional joy from being with Shirley, the secretary. As a married man, Pastor Alonzo believed his relationship with Shirley had become inappropriate even though he had carefully guarded the relationship from becoming sexual. "I'm an emotional adulterer," he hesitantly confessed.

"He's a pervert," Larry reported to the Board of Elders. "And I want him out of here." The church became hopelessly entangled in dissention and controversy in response to the self-disclosure. Pastor Alonzo was able to retain his position, but he never regained his former status as a spiritual leader. Some simply failed to understand him, others believed he was involved in ongoing sin.

Guerra (2001) acknowledges that pastoral self-disclosure where personal sin is at issue must be handled carefully. "To say that you do not struggle is to be a liar, but to say that you're not winning in the struggle is to be disqualified" (p. 59).

Stowell (2001) notes with regard to the same issue that a pastor will assume one of two roles for the flock. Either he or she will be an example to better living or an excuse for poor living. He suggests four important ways to do pastoral self-disclosure while continuing the role of example rather than excuse.

1. Don't repeatedly dwell on the same category of failure.
2. Don't trivialize failure.
3. Emphasize solutions, not struggles.

4. Offset spiritual failure with spiritual success in the content of any self-disclosure. (p. 59)

ENCOURAGING OTHERS TO SELF-DISCLOSE

As a spiritual leader and people helper, the effective pastor must be interested in not only personal self-disclosure, but also in how to help others self-disclose appropriately and effectively. Whether in the counseling room, boardroom, or in any number of other dyadic situations, certain phrases encourage self-disclosure and others discourage people from revealing their inner feelings. Some phrases that encourage self-disclosure include

- Would you like to talk about it?
- How do you feel about that?
- That must be exciting (or discouraging, frustrating, thrilling, encouraging) to you.
- I'd love to hear about it.
- Have you ever had an experience such as that before?
- Tell me more.
- What do you think about that?
- Then what happened?

Some phrases serve to end conversation and discourage others from self-disclosure. Samples of these phrases include

- Don't worry. I'm sure it will work out.
- How could you possibly feel that way?
- I've really got to run.
- That reminds me of the time when . . .
- Things like that happen to everyone.
- You should have . . .

The effective pastor will want to select phrases from the list that encourage self-disclosure as much as possible. In addition to using these encouraging phrases and other similar ones, the effective pastoral communicator will want to develop skills in appropriate personal self-disclosure. That way self-disclosure becomes a useful and vital part of pastoral communication, and those in relationship with the pastor feel free to reveal their innermost selves.

KEY CONCEPTS

Self-disclosure occurs when a communicator intentionally reveals the aspects of his or her personal life that another person could not reasonably be expected to discover on his or her own. Some of the reasons for self-disclosure include

- Catharsis
- Self-projection
- Self-clarification
- Reciprocity
- Relationship enhancement

Many pastors fail to self-disclose in order to avoid the inherent risks in the process, because they assume no one is interested, or because they honestly do not know how to self-disclose safely and effectively.

MEANINGS MANIA

Word Bank

    a. self-disclosure
    b. self-validation
    c. cliché
    d. self-clarification
    e. peak communication
    f. Johari window

Definitions

_____ 1. A four-quadrant diagram that helps explain self-disclosure
_____ 2. A word or phrase that has little real meaning and hence is at the first level of communication

_____ 3. Disclosure designed to enhance the image of the discloser
_____ 4. Open sharing of innermost secrets
_____ 5. Self-disclosure designed to internally confirm a belief or validate a behavior
_____ 6. Intentionally telling another person things about yourself that he or she could not reasonably discover any other way

UNLEASHING THE POWER
OF INTERPERSONAL COMMUNICATION

Draw a window similar to the one shown in Figure 4.1 in order to analyze your relationship with your best friend on the subject of "a call to ministry." Be certain to indicate the appropriate relative size of the four panes. How would the window differ with that same person on the subject of "sin in believers"? How would the window differ with that same person on the subject of "my earliest memories"? How would those three windows change with a different person?

Chapter 5

Verbal Messages

"Not one of us in the Hollow will be speaking to you now. You may not eat at the same table as church members or do business with any of us . . ." In the painful hours that followed, not only did Katie's entire family nix any conversation with her, they also refused to accept written notes from her. (Lewis, 1997, p. 229)

Lewis is describing shunning, the Amish practice of isolating those believed to be in sin. Later in the same novel she illustrates the powerful effects of shunning. "Suddenly she knew the meaning of the word alone. Knew it more powerfully than she'd ever known anything" (p. 238).

Of course the aloneness that comes with shunning is designed to hasten a return to spiritual obedience. But studies indicate that isolation may provoke other more negative results. For example, medical scientists have long maintained a link between psychosocial influences and coronary heart disease (Williams and Chesney, 1993). Both Hall and Havens (2001) and Auslander and Litwin (1995) demonstrate that loneliness can lead to more negative reports of general health in older adults, and the BBC (2002) reports that children living in isolated rural areas may be at greater risk of developing diabetes. Karren et al. (2002), in their comprehensive study on the effects of attitudes as well as relationships on health, report a correlation between loneliness and general health. Clearly isolation can have serious health consequences.

This may be one of the reasons for God's appraisal in Genesis 2:18, "It is not good for the man to be alone. . . ." Avoidance of such serious consequences may be the reason that over time verbal systems of interaction have developed among human beings.

THE NATURE OF WORDS

Verbal communication is the process of using language in order to avoid isolation by sending and receiving messages. Language is a system developed through the use of words and their combinations. Effective pastoral communicators must understand the following six parameters, which combine to establish the nature of words.

Words Are Symbolic

Most words have no meaning within themselves. A word is only an arbitrary symbol that has meaning because of consensual validation or the agreement of a group on a particular meaning. For example, the word "Bible" may mean different things to different people.

- To Jan, a protestant clergywoman, the term denotes the sixty-six canonical books of sacred writ.
- For Ron, a Roman Catholic layman, the term also includes the Apocryphal books.
- To Shawn, a fundamentalist Christian, only the King James Version is the true Bible.
- But Lisa, a recently confirmed member of a mainline church, associates the term with her copy of a modern translation in contemporary language.

Sometimes two communicators use the same word but are ascribing two different meanings to it. As a result the two fail to effectively communicate because of what is called bypassing. Bypassing, the communication problem that occurs when two people use the same word or phrase but assign different meanings to it, is illustrated in Pastoral Conversation 5.1.

Pastoral Conversation 5.1

Background

Anne is the secretary of the Administrative Council at Good Shepherd Church where Michelle is pastor. Anne often works second shift in her job and doesn't usually get up until 9:00 a.m. or after. By contrast, Pastor Michelle has discovered that she accomplishes a great deal more and thinks more clearly in the early morning. She often is in the church office by 5:00 a.m., but returns home for a mid-morning brunch at 9:00 a.m. In a telephone conversation the following exchange took place between the two.

Dialogue

ANNE: Pastor, I've finished typing the minutes of last week's Ad Council meeting and wondered when I might drop them off for you to proofread.

PASTOR MICHELLE: Any time is fine, Anne.

ANNE: I'll bring them by first thing in the morning then.

PASTOR MICHELLE: Wonderful.

Analysis

1. What time is first thing in the morning to Anne? What time does that mean to Michelle?
2. What are the possible outcomes of this proposed meeting?
3. How could bypassing have been avoided in this brief exchange?

Words Are Cultural

Culture is the term given to the rules, norms, values, and expectations that surround a particular society or group. Words also derive a great deal of their meaning from the culture in which they are used. This truth is obvious when applied to words from different languages, but words derive much of their meaning from culture even within the same language.

Pastor Pat discovered that words were cultural when he moved from his lifelong home in the Midwest to a new pastorate in the South. He noted a strange response from Tina, one of the teens in the youth group, when he ordered a "pop" at the church social. An older member of the congregation explained to Tina that Pastor Pat was a "Yankee." The information seemed to clarify for Tina, but it left Pastor Pat even more confused. At issue was the fact that pop is a term, culturally adapted by folks primarily in the Midwest, to describe soft drinks. Tina would undoubtedly use the term "coke" to describe the same product, regardless of brand preference. In addition, Tina took "Yankee" to mean a person from the North, and Pastor Pat immediately thought of the baseball team.

Pastors do well to remember the cultural nature of words. This is especially true when they attempt to discuss theological issues with laypeople. Growing out of the culture of Bible college or seminary is an entire lexicon of theological terms or jargon. Those words may have different meanings or no meaning at all for those less familiar with that specialized culture.

Words Are Contextual

In addition to deriving their meaning from culture, words depend to a large extent upon the context in which they are used. The phrase, "How are you doing?" may be a simple greeting similar to "Hello," when spoken to a stranger on the street. When spoken to a parishioner in a hospital emergency room, however, the same phrase takes on a whole new depth of meaning.

Uproar developed at Calvary Church when word spread that Pastor Kyle would present plans to the Administrative Council for moving the church. The church had been at the same location for nearly 100 years, and many were outraged at the notion. Later, however, it was discovered that the entire misunderstanding had developed when Pastor Kyle was overheard making plans with the chairperson of evangelism to present a program to "get the church moving." The context in which words are spoken is very important.

Words Are Abstract

Words do not have any comprehensive, agreed upon meaning. In nearly every case words can have two or more possible meanings. Thus it can be said that the words themselves are abstract. At a minimum, every word has at least a denotative and a connotative meaning.

Denotative meanings are the literal, dictionary meaning of a word. Connotative meanings are the personal and subjective meanings that abide within an individual. The denotative meaning of the word "church" might be a building used for public worship. This definition hardly is sufficient, however, to describe what is meant when the term "church" is spoken by individuals such as the following:

- a ninety-year-old woman who has been a member of the same congregation since she was a small child;
- a struggling teen who has just been invited by a peer to the youth fellowship;
- a pastor who has experienced recent undeserved criticism from members of his congregation; or
- a single mother who just dropped her kids off for Sunday school.

Each of these people has a unique connotative meaning for the same term.

Connotative meaning has caused some communication experts to declare that words don't mean things; people mean things (Griffin, 1987). Since the connotative meaning is not the same for any two communicators, it is not the words that are important but the meaning a person has for the word. Perhaps a better way to express the truth would be to note that words mean so many things that it is important for a communicator to search for the intended meaning.

Laswell and Laswell (1976) explored what subjects meant when they used the term "love." They discovered at least six different meanings for that simple word.

- For some, the word love could best be translated as "lifelong friends." Even in romantic dyads, this definition reflects those who are most like siblings in their relationship.
- For others, to be in love is to be totally other-oriented. The biblical concept of agape matches their understanding of a loving relationship.
- Some love in an extremely possessive and dependent way. Their understanding of love is exclusive and jealous in nature.
- Others use the word love with regard to a very pragmatic, logical, and sensible agenda within the relationship. They choose a lover on the basis of what makes sense.
- Those who are self-centered in their approach make up a fifth group of understandings about love. These lovers may record love relationships similar to notches on a belt.
- Finally, those with a romantic understanding of love are whole-person lovers. They believe in love at first sight and may become physically ill at the other person's absence.

The Laswell and Laswell work is instructive for pastors in two important ways. First, it helps to point out the abstract nature of words. But perhaps just as important are the specific revelations of the study on the word love, which is a much-used Christian term. Every parishioner will not have the same understanding when the pastor uses the word love or similar abstract terms.

Words Are Gender Oriented

Within a culture men and women presumably speak the same language. Yet careful observation reveals that there are striking differences in the way men and women use words (Tannen, 1990). These differences must be understood by effective pastors of either gender in order to avoid frustrations when communicating with parishioners of the opposite gender.

Women generally measure the success of interpersonal relationships on the basis of conversation. They see talk as the essence of the relationship (Wood, 2005). Men see conversation as a tool with which to accomplish a task. In addition, they use words as a means of exerting control. The relational aspects of talk are much less important to male conversationalists (Adler and Towne, 2003). Tannen (1990) suggests that these differences begin very early when boys talk to exert control over playmates, while girls talk in order to maintain tranquility. Kohn (1988) has summarized the research of language differences between boys and girls and drawn similar conclusions.

Some believe that the lack of power or control talk by women is a function of their historic role in society. Others take less of a victimization approach, noting that what is lost by women in powerlessness is more than compensated for in the ability to build rapport in a relationship (Tannen, 1994). Pastors of both genders must recognize the differences in the way men and women communicate and attempt to translate appropriately and effectively when conversing with colleagues and parishioners of the opposite gender.

Words Are Powerful

The expression, "sticks and stones may break my bones, but words can never hurt me," was obviously first uttered by a person who had never experienced the pain of an inappropriate or unkind word. The truth is that words are extremely powerful. They do have the power to hurt or the power to help. Sometimes it is difficult to tell whether words are being used in a helpful or hurtful way, which is the situation in Pastoral Conversation 5.2.

Pastoral Conversation 5.2

Background

Pastor Terry has just returned from a week-long vacation with his family. He is especially anxious to hear how the Sunday morning service went with Reverend Engels, a retired pastor from the area, doing the pulpit supply. Pastor Terry has called Jeff Fender for an update. A portion of their conversation appears below.

Dialogue

PASTOR TERRY: Hi, Jeff! This is Pastor Terry.

JEFF: Hi, Pastor. Welcome home. How was the vacation?

PASTOR TERRY: It was wonderful. I was concerned about Sunday morning, though. How did Reverend Engels do?

JEFF: No need to worry. He did a great job. In fact, I heard several say that it was the best sermon they had heard preached from that pulpit in a long time.

Analysis

1. Did Jeff intend for his report to help Pastor Terry by putting his mind at ease, or did he intend a negative evaluation of Pastor Terry's preaching? How do you know?
2. What would you suggest Pastor Terry say in response?
3. Why would Jeff make his report in such a way? What other examples have you seen of carelessly spoken words?

In addition to the power to hurt or help, the Genesis account reveals that words have the power to shape and develop culture. According to Genesis 11, the dispersion of people into various cultural and ethnic groups came about as a result of language. Modern language theorists support the possibility. Among them, Whorf, who along with colleague Sapir, developed the Sapir-Whorf hypothesis (Whorf and Carroll, 1998). They believe that language and thinking are so inter-related that thought is actually rooted in language. That is to say, a person cannot conceive of that for which there are no words. Words have great power to shape the very nature of the society.

Understanding the six word parameters gives the pastoral communicator a better understanding of the nature of language. What the effective pastor must also realize, however, is that some words are simply better not spoken.

GOSSIP: A WORD BETTER LEFT UNSPOKEN

Gossip refers to idle talk or rumors about a third party. Laing (1993) argues that gossip is a near universal practice and serves the positive function of socialization. DeVito (2000) maintains that "to advise anyone not to gossip would be absurd" (p. 126). Gossip is strictly forbidden in scripture and is nearly always detrimental to pastoral effectiveness.

James wrote to his followers with a vivid imagery when he said, "The tongue also is a fire, a world of evil among the parts of the body" (James 3:6). Paul puts the gossiper in a long list of evildoers. "They are gossips, slanderers, God-haters, insolent, arrogant and boastful; they invent ways of doing evil . . ." (Romans 1:29-30). He later condemns such behaviors harshly be saying, "those who do such things deserve death . . ." (Romans 1:32).

Although falling short of these scriptural standards, DeVito (2000, p. 126) offers three ethical tests of gossip. He maintains that gossip is best avoided if it encompasses a subject that

- includes information that a communicator promised to keep secret;
- invades the privacy of an individual; and
- is known to be false.

The words of Jesus are perhaps the most poignant on the subject. In a postresurrection conversation with Peter, Jesus reveals Peter's future service to the kingdom and the suffering he must endure. Perhaps uncomfortable with the spotlight, Peter points to John and asks, "Lord, what about him?" (John 21:21).

Jesus' response becomes a measuring stick for every pastor to use in determining whether a topic should be addressed or left out of the conversation. His rebuke in the form of a rhetorical question was, "What is that to you?" (John 21:22). That is precisely the question every pastor should mentally ask before uttering an idle or malicious word.

In the process of practicing the "What is that to you?" standard, effective pastoral communicators will need to take great care to avoid three myths that frequently surround the practice of gossip.

Myth 1: It's Not Gossip if It's True

Jesus could have told Peter the truth in response to his question about John. He did not answer because he refused to gossip, not because he refused to tell falsehoods. Of course pastors should never engage in falsehoods. But even some truths are better left unsaid.

Myth 2: It's Not Gossip if I Only Tell One

Telling just one is precisely what Peter asked of Jesus, since they were presumably engaged in a private conversation. Jesus could have told Peter what he wanted him to know and then simply cautioned him to tell no one else. But, to have done so would have been to gossip. Jesus chose not to participate.

Myth 3: It's Not Gossip; It's a Prayer Concern

This myth is perhaps the most insidious of the three because it uses spiritual discipline as the rationale for the performance of evil. God's people do not need to know every detail of a situation in order to pray effectively. Jesus might well have responded to Peter's request for information and then added, "Peter, I'm glad you ask. Now you will be able to pray more intelligently." Jesus chose, however, a higher standard. He elected not to gossip.

Pastors should strive to employ the "What is that to you?" standard to their personal and professional conversations. Anything less weakens pastoral effectiveness. Gossip is simply a word that should not be spoken.

CONFIDENTIALITY: A LIMIT ON PASTORAL WORDS

In addition to avoiding gossip, pastors must avoid the disclosure of information that they have learned in confidence. Forty-nine states have statutes that legally safeguard a pastor from being forced to testify to privileged information in a court of law (Tiemann and Bush, 1983). In most cases, these cover information that comes in the form of confession, pastoral counseling, or other professional capacity. Recent trends allow for clergy silence in less penitential situations.

The definition of confidential communication offered to counselors by Clinton and Ohlschlager (2002) applies to pastors as well. They include as confidential "all verbal, written, telephonic, audio or video taped, or electronic communications arising within the helping relationship" (p. 262). In general, pastors should assume that whatever they know about the personal lives of their parishioners must not be divulged to another except under three important circumstances.

Exception 1: Informed Consent

A widely recognized exception to the general rules of confidentiality involves those cases where the parishioner grants permission for disclosure. Pastors must take care to ascertain that the parishioner understands the full ramifications of his or her consent and in many cases should obtain written permission as legal protection.

Pastor Gary was called to testify in a court of law with regard to a child custody dispute. In that capacity, Pastor Gary had to reveal information about a parishioner's abilities as a parent. Even though he had never counseled the parishioner formally, what he knew of her parental abilities he had obtained as a result of pastoral visits in the home and professional observations at the church. Pastor Gary wisely requested permission to reveal the information. The parishioner readily granted the permission since Pastor Gary's opinion at the hearing would be positive and helpful. In many cases the matter of informed consent is not so easily handled.

Sometimes informed consent is much less formal, but no less significant. Pastor Shawn knew in his capacity as youth pastor that one of his teenage parishioners planned to prepare for a career in missions. When a potential employer called for a reference, Pastor Shawn proudly mentioned the teen's plans. The revelation cost the parishioner the job since the employer was not interested in hiring someone who would be leaving in a few years. Further, Pastor Shawn had no defense, legal or otherwise, when confronted by the angry teenager for his breach of confidentiality.

Sometimes there is a question about whether information a pastor has is privileged or simply routine. That was the case when Pastor Eileen learned of a physical need of Sara. Sara was both Eileen's hairdresser and a parishioner. In the beauty shop one day, when no other clients were present, Sara mentioned the ongoing physical ailment. Before leaving, Pastor Eileen clarified, "Is it okay for me to tell the Thursday afternoon prayer group about your problem?" The resultant informal, but important, informed consent paved the way for mention of the prayer request. In addition, the request for permission gave Sara a new confidence in her pastor's high standards of confidentiality. Wise is the pastor who assumes that everything he or she knows is confidential, until an informed consent is received.

Exception 2: Self-Harm

A second exception to the rule that everything a pastor knows is confidential involves those situations where a parishioner may inflict self-harm. When a parishioner intends to harm himself or herself the pastor has an ethical obligation to reveal the intent to an appropriate third party. Even under these circumstances, the revelation must be limited to those who have the ability to help. The revelation should never be to the community at large.

Jeff was a young adult in the church shepherded by Pastor Carole. In a conversation with Pastor Carole, Jeff revealed his suicidal inclinations. Pastor Carole asked a few questions to determine in her own mind the nature of the risk. She then phoned authorities, which put Jeff in protective care in spite of his objections. Pastor Carole refused to discuss the matter with anyone else in the congregation.

One question that often arises as pastors determine whether or not to disclose involves the nature and immediacy of the intent to harm, which is the issue in Pastoral Conversation 5.3. One might legitimately argue that Veronica is not harming herself at all if it proves that she does not have cancer. But then again, what if she does have the disease?

Pastoral Conversation 5.3

Background

Pastor Myron responded to the doorbell at the parsonage one Saturday afternoon. At the door was Veronica Mills, a retired schoolteacher and active participant at Calvary Church. When Pastor Myron welcomed Veronica inside, the following conversation took place.

Dialogue

VERONICA: Pastor, before I tell you why I've come, I want to make absolutely sure that you won't tell anyone what I am about to say. I realize that you know my children, and I don't want them to find out.

PASTOR MYRON: Of course, Veronica. What is it?

VERONICA: I have a fairly large lump on my breast that has been growing for several weeks. I think I have cancer, but I'm too scared to even think of going to the doctor.

Analysis

1. Does this situation fall under the self-harm exclusion to confidentiality? Defend your answer.
2. What should Pastor Myron say at this point to Veronica?
3. How could Pastor Myron have avoided this uncomfortable ethical dilemma?

Exception 3: Duty to Protect

A third exception to the pastor's responsibility to complete confidentiality is when there exists a threat to a third party. Experts agree and courts have upheld that professionals have a duty to protect an unsuspecting or innocent third party.

Collins (1990) describes the circumstances of the landmark case *Tarasoff v. Regents of the University of California*. A patient who was being treated by a California psychologist killed Tatiana Tarasoff. The psychologist knew of the patient's obsession with Tarasoff and recognized that the patient was dangerous. He refused to warn Tarasoff, however, believing his responsibility to client confidentiality took precedence. After Tarisoff's murder her parents sued the psychologist and his employer.

> The court ruled that a counselor must use "reasonable care" to protect an intended victim when the counselor "determines, or pursuant to the standards of his profession should determine, that the patient presents a serious danger of violence to another." (Collins, 1990, p. 33)

Pastors and others in helping professions should follow a similar guideline with regard to information they may have learned in confidence.

The duty to protect exclusion is multifaceted. For example, most states have laws requiring pastors to report any case of suspected child abuse. And increasingly it is anticipated that those in helping professions would warn the spouse of an AIDS victim with or without that victim's permission (Pietrofesa, Pietrofesa, and Pietrofesa, 1990).

Such situations will require a pastor to make judgments about the likelihood and degree of potential harm. The general rule of confidentiality may not be blindly followed in the twenty-first century. The complexities of the culture make exceptions to the confidentiality mandate quite common.

KEY CONCEPTS

The verbal message system is the one most commonly used among communicators to send and receive messages. Verbal message systems are comprised of language, and words are the building blocks of language. Pastoral communicators should understand six important parameters about the nature of words. Words are:

1. Symbolic
2. Cultural
3. Contextual
4. Abstract
5. Gender-oriented
6. Powerful

The powerful nature of words makes it essential that pastors use them appropriately. Gossip is never an appropriate use of words. Some attempt to defend poor conversational practices by suggesting that it is not gossip if it is true, only told once, or only told as a prayer request. Instead, effective pastoral communicators utilize the "What is that to you?" standard.

Finally, the appropriate use of words raises issues concerning confidentiality. Pastors have a right to maintain silence, and parishioners have a right to expect their communiqués with their pastor to be held in strict confidence with three notable exceptions. These are:

- Informed consent
- Self-harm
- Duty to protect

MEANINGS MANIA

Word Bank

a. verbal communication
b. gossip
c. duty to protect
d. Sapir-Whorf hypothesis
e. informed consent
f. words

Definitions

_____ 1. Maintains that thought is rooted in language
_____ 2. Idle talk or rumors about a third party
_____ 3. Permission to disclose confidential information with the full understanding of the ramifications

_____ 4. Communication by means of language
_____ 5. The building blocks of language
_____ 6. Responsibility of a professional to warn the innocent or
unsuspecting

UNLEASHING THE POWER
OF INTERPERSONAL COMMUNICATION

Select a partner and take turns defining the following terms. Record your responses.

1. Love
2. Peace
3. Joy
4. Hope
5. Happiness
6. Humility
7. Kindness
8. Meanness
9. Evil
10. Wisdom

Now look up the definition for each word in a dictionary. How does your connotative meaning differ from the denotative meaning? How does your partner's connotative meaning differ? How can the use of this knowledge improve your power of communication?

Chapter 6

Nonverbal Messages

Captain Eugene McDaniel (1975) reports that in a Vietnamese prisoner-of-war camp the potential negative impact of the lack of communication became a life and death issue. Both the American prisoners and their North Vietnamese captors knew that a person could stand more pain when linked with others. Thus while the North Vietnamese attempted to enforce complete isolation, Captain McDaniel and his cocaptives developed sophisticated and often dangerous systems for sending and receiving unspoken messages. Outside the prisoner-of-war camp and in more typical circumstances the sending and receiving of messages is sometimes accomplished by means of verbal communication as discussed in Chapter 5. But at other times messages are sent and received through nonverbal communication.

Words do have power, but observers conclude that the nonverbal message system may have an even greater power. "Some social scientists have argued that 93 percent of the emotional impact of a message comes from nonverbal sources. Others have reasoned more convincingly that the figure is closer to 65 percent" (Adler and Towne, 2003, p. 223). Regardless of the precise figure, it is clear that a large part of the emotional impact of a message is borne through nonverbal communication (Burgoon, 1994). The effective pastor will need to have a clear understanding of the role of the nonverbal message system.

Nonverbal communication is "communication other than written or spoken language that creates meaning for someone" (Beebe, Beebe, and Ivy, 2001, p. 88). Typically, nonverbal communication is considered according to a series of classifications or types. These include appearance, gestures and body movements, facial expressions and eye behavior, vocalics, space and territoriality, touch, and time.

APPEARANCE

Americans place a very high value on physical attractiveness. Millions of dollars are spent annually for cosmetics, hair care products, diet aids, and designer clothing in order to project a more appealing image. Research demonstrates that Americans tend to think of those who are attractive as also more credible, happy, popular, and prosperous than those less attractive (Beebe, Beebe, and Ivy, 2001). In addition, attractive students receive higher grades, attractive people are more persuasive, and attractive people are more likely to get the job (Richmond and McCroskey, 2000).

One aspect of physical attractiveness involves body shape and size. Sheldon (1940), a pioneer in the work of nonverbal communication through body type, suggests that there are three major body types. The *endomorph* is a rounded, oval-shaped body type. Endomorphs are usually heavier, though not necessarily overweight. Others view them as calm, relaxed, tolerant, generous, and kind. *Mesomorphs* have a more triangular body shape. They appear more firm and muscular, being broad at the shoulders and narrow at the hips. People view mesomorphs as dominant, confident, competitive, adventurous, assertive, and optimistic. Finally, *ectomorphic* body types are thin and tall. They are viewed as having a fragile-looking physique. Emotionally ectomorphs are viewed as tense, meticulous, introspective, cautious, and sensitive. Pastors should beware of stereotyping people according to these body types and then reacting toward them on the basis of these stereotypical expectations.

In addition to body shape, clothing and other artifacts including jewelry, makeup, cologne, and eyeglasses all communicate nonverbally to others. Dressing as others do and thus creating a perceived similarity can be beneficial to interpersonal relationships. When Pastor Mike moved from a suburban church to a small-town environment he discovered that adding jeans to his wardrobe helped him gain acceptance from members of the congregation.

Pastor Joan wore a clerical collar as she moved among the members of her community. She recognized that symbolic clothing serves to enhance rank or status.

Pastor Greg wore business suits seven days a week in his interaction with parishioners. The congregation he served was largely made up of highly successful business and professional people. Pastor Greg knew that experts have concluded that a man's business suit sends messages of authority and credibility (Richmond and McCroskey, 2000).

GESTURES AND BODY MOVEMENTS

A heightened awareness of "body language" as it is sometimes called has developed as a result of the appearance of popular literature on the subject. Although some of this awareness is positive, much has caused observers to misinterpret or overinterpret every body movement. For example, communicators may be reluctant to fold their arms during a conversation for fear of being interpreted as closing out the speaker. On the other hand, there is some benefit from a general understanding of the study of human movements, gestures, and posture, or kinesics as that study is called.

Various scholars have attempted to categorize kinesics. None have gained the widespread acceptance of Ekman and Friesen (1969), who suggest five kinesic categories according to their functions. These are emblems, illustrators, affect displays, regulators, and adaptors.

Emblems are nonverbal cues that actually substitute for a word or phrase. When Pastor Clay peeked through the door of the sixth grade boys Sunday school classroom he put his index finger to pursed lips without making a sound or saying a word. Pastor Clay had used an emblem.

Illustrators are nonverbal behaviors that accompany a verbal message and usually seek to enhance or complement the message. Pointing while giving verbal directions is a common example. Pastor Josh noted that he had to get going because he had three hospital calls to make. Holding up three fingers for emphasis served as an illustrator for Pastor Josh's comment.

Affect displays are those nonverbal cues that communicate emotion. Facial expressions can reveal happiness or sadness. Body language can reveal the degree of the emotion. Therefore, a sad face with slumped shoulders communicates sadness with a great deal of intensity. Pastor Chad read the affect displays being emanated from the youth pastor at his church. Without even being told, he correctly guessed, "You had a great response to the youth retreat." Not only was Pastor Chad correct in his assessment, he was also viewed by the youth pastor as a very astute observer.

Regulators control the flow of communication and are usually less conscious than the other kinesic categories. A person who is eager to respond may take in a breath, lean forward, or raise an eyebrow. One who does not wish to speak may avert eye contact, cross his or her arms, or respond with a simple, "uh-huh."

Adaptors are unintentional nonverbal behaviors that help a communicator satisfy a personal need and adapt to a situation. Foot tapping to relieve stress is a common example. Hair pulling that demonstrates contemplation is another.

FACIAL EXPRESSIONS AND EYE BEHAVIOR

Facial expressions communicate a broad range of emotions and reactions. The human face is capable of producing 250,000 different expressions (Ekman and Friesen, 1975). Eight emotions displayed on the face are considered primary, however. They are referred to as primary affect displays and include happiness, surprise, fear, anger, sadness, disgust, contempt, and interest (Ekman and Friesen, 1975).

Messages communicated by the eyes comprise a study known as *oculesis*. In American culture the average length of a gaze is 2.95 seconds when the gaze is one-directional, but the average time that two persons gaze at each other is 1.18 seconds (Argyle, 1990). Eye contact short of these averages communicates a lack of interest, a preoccupation, or excessive shyness. An excessive gaze may show unusually high or even inappropriate interest.

Duration and direction of gaze are both voluntarily controlled by a communicator. Another aspect of oculesis, pupil dilation, cannot be controlled. Pupils enlarge when a listener is interested in something or is emotionally aroused. In addition, dilated pupils are judged more attractive than smaller ones (Marshall, 1983). Noting the changes in the pupil size of others usually occurs at a subconscious level.

VOCALICS

Vocalics, or paralanguage as it is sometimes called, refers to the vocal but nonverbal aspects of speech. As such, it is a specialized form of nonverbal communication. Such vocal characteristics as pitch, rate, emphasis, or volume all communicate various meanings even though the same words are used.

Consider a different emphasis on each of four words in the following sentence. Notice how the meaning changes with just the shift in emphasis.

1. Do *you* attend that church?
2. Do you *attend* that church?
3. Do you attend *that* church?
4. Do you attend that *church*?

One specialized study within vocalics considers the impact of silence in communication. Pausing or remaining silent can often communicate volumes. Silence may be used to avoid or prevent certain communication. Pastor Diana was confronted about the rumor around the church that she was contemplating resigning her position. She silently shrugged in response. As a result, the chairperson of the Administrative Council concluded that the rumor was indeed true. Pastor Diana's silence had spoken.

SPACE AND TERRITORIALITY

A person's use of space, technically called proxemics, communicates a great deal about him or her. So, too, does the territory one occupies or owns. In his foundational work on spatial distances, Hall (1966) noted four zones that reveal the type of relationship people are in, and the types of communication that they are likely to engage in.

The *intimate zone* ranges from the point of touching to one-and-a-half feet. This zone is reserved for those with whom a communicator has the closest possible relationship and is regarded by most people as inappropriate in public. Only very personal conversation occurs in the intimate zone. One of the reasons many people find elevators uncomfortable is that it allows strangers in this intimate space.

The second spatial zone, ranging from one-and-a-half feet to four feet, Hall called *personal space*. This is used for conversations with family members and friends. Personal space can be thought of as a protective bubble. Others usually enter the bubble only by mutual agreement.

The *social zone,* from four to twelve feet, is where formal exchanges and professional interactions occur. Often professionals arrange their desk and other office furniture so as to guarantee these distances.

The fourth zone, commonly referred to as the *public zone,* begins at about twelve feet and extends as far as interaction is possible. Little interpersonal communication takes place in this zone. Instead, it is the realm of much public address.

Questions of propriety in interpersonal communication will consider these four spatial zones. Such questions take on added dimensions for those engaged in the business of pastoral ministry. For example, is it appropriate for a pastor to enter the intimate range of a parishioner as a form of greeting? That is the question of Pastoral Conversation 6.1.

Pastoral Conversation 6.1

Background

Pastor Kevin has been at St. James Church for six months. He is extremely outgoing and friendly. In most matters he has been very well received by the parishioners. Some laypeople, however, have discussed Pastor Kevin's practice of greeting people on Sunday morning with a friendly hug. The matter came to the fore one Sunday when Pastor Kevin approached Brett, a regular attendee at the church. Pastor Kevin had stretched his arms as if to hug Brett.

Dialogue

BRETT: (extending his right hand) I'm a handshaker myself.

PASTOR KEVIN: Excuse me?

BRETT: I said I'm a handshaker, not a hugger. And I think there are some others like that around the church.

Pastor Kevin, a bit taken aback, stood for a moment with his arms outstretched while Brett stood with his arm extended.

Analysis

1. Is Pastor Kevin's greeting style appropriate? Does the age of the recipient of his hug make a difference? Does the gender of the recipient matter? Does the setting change the answer (i.e., Sunday worship, administrative meeting, hospital corridor)?
2. How should Pastor Kevin greet Brett right now? What should he say and do the next time he greets Brett?
3. Should this encounter affect the way Pastor Kevin greets the other parishioners? Explain your answer.

As pastors seek to answer the questions raised in Pastoral Conversation 6.1 and others similar to them, several observations concerning interpersonal space may prove helpful (Sommer, 1959; Reinland and Jones, 1995; Hickman and Stacks, 1993).

1. The more a communicator likes someone, the closer he or she stands.
2. Higher-status persons are given more space.
3. A larger room draws people closer together.
4. Women stand closer to others than men do.
5. When discussing personal topics, people stand closer together.
6. As people age their spaces become larger.
7. People maintain greater distances from those they see as different from themselves or whom they evaluate negatively.

TOUCH

Haptics, or the study of touch, may also bring to bear some information related to Pastor Kevin's practice of hugging and Brett's reaction. Touch can carry a wide variety of messages as noted by Jones and Yarbrough (1985, pp. 20-22).

- Touch can communicate positive feelings of support, trust, or appreciation. (p. 30)
- Touch can be playful. (p. 32)
- Touch can control. It sometimes says, "Stop that!" or "Move over." (p. 32)

- Touch can be ritualistic as with a greeting or a good-bye. (p. 34)
- Touch can be task-related. For example, this occurs when help-ing someone up the stairs. (p. 35)

In Pastoral Conversation 6.1, Pastor Kevin saw touch in ritualistic terms. He felt that the hug was preferable to the handshake among members of a church family. Brett interpreted the touch in terms of positive feelings. He believed that Pastor Kevin was communicating affection or trust, when in fact he believed that their relationship was too young for such a message.

Jesus' ministry often involved touch. On one occasion he healed a blind man's eyes by means of mud and physical touch. On the night he was betrayed, with a touch he healed the ear of Malchus after Pe-ter's violent outburst with a sword. On one occasion the touch was initiated by a sick woman rather than by the great physician. Yet, even on this occasion Jesus expressed tremendous sensitivity to touch when he asked, "Who touched me?" (Luke 8:45). Presumably the question was not designed as a rebuke, but as an acknowledgement.

In today's high-tech but low-touch culture effective pastors utilize an appropriate ministry of touch. A hand on the shoulder of a grieving spouse offers the comfort of presence in a difficult situation. "Giving five" to the youngest members of the congregation communicates that the leader of the people of God is a part of the real world, even that world in which boys and girls live. Perhaps the greatest, yet fre-quently overlooked, opportunity for touch takes place in the hospital room, where the pastor makes a call. In Pastoral Conversation 6.2, Pastor Tyler learns about the power of touch from a parishioner.

Pastoral Conversation 6.2

Background

Pastor Tyler is about to leave the hospital room of Frank Garrett. Associate Pastor Howard made a call in Frank's room yesterday. Af-ter a prayer, but before Pastor Tyler excuses himself, the following di-alogue takes place.

Dialogue

FRANK: Pastor, I want you to know how much I appreciate your visit and your prayer.

PASTOR TYLER: It's good to visit and pray with you, Frank. I'm delighted at your improvement.

FRANK: Yesterday, when Pastor Howard was here, it made me realize how much I appreciate your ministry style.

PASTOR TYLER: Oh?

FRANK: He's a nice kid, and he prayed for me too. But, I guess he is just too professional or something. I really appreciate the way you take my hand when we pray. It makes me feel like I'm not alone in this place.

Analysis

1. How should Pastor Tyler respond to Frank? What care must he take to support his colleague and subordinate, Pastor Howard? Is Frank's statement really about Pastor Howard at all?
2. How do you explain the power of touch in a hospital sickroom? How did Frank explain it?
3. Is it ever inappropriate for a pastor to take the hand of a parishioner when praying? Support your answer with examples.
4. What if anything should Pastor Tyler say about this conversation to Pastor Howard? Support your response.

TIME

Chronemics is the study of how time affects messages. Specifically, the study explores how communicators partition time into past, present, and future. Those with past orientation have a special reverence for the past. They relive old times as the "good old days." Present-oriented people live for the day. They see the past as merely history, having little or no bearing on the present. The future, they argue, may never come. By contrast, future-oriented people live for the future. They save, work hard, and deny themselves today in order to adequately prepare for the future.

These three basic time orientations impact the way people think and communicate. The wise pastor carefully listens for the time orientation of others in order to better understand their points of view and thus enhance communication. Consider Pastor Jeff's interaction with three members of his church's governing body. The committee has agreed that something has to be done to curb the steady, twenty-year decline in membership and attendance. Three main positions on what to do are evident in the committee. These follow the time orientations of the various members.

- *Past oriented.* Parishioner Edward has a past orientation. He suggests, "We need to take a careful look at what made this church great in the past. A survey of our oldest members would help us discover the reason for our recent decline."
- *Present oriented.* Evelyn is a member of the committee with a present orientation. She articulates her position by saying, "It is not about the past and it's not about the future. We need to develop the programs and ministries that will bring people into the church now. If we're going to survey anyone, we should ask our neighbors what we could do to involve them."
- *Future oriented.* Janice is future orientated. Her solution thus involves vision. She declares, "Without a vision statement and a plan for the future we'll just continue to spiral down. Children's ministries are vital because kids are the church of tomorrow. If we're going to save the church for the next generation we need to think long-term."

By recognizing the time orientations behind comments such as these, Pastor Jeff will be more likely to help the group arrive at a working solution to the dilemma of what to do about the declining church. He may need to search for a compromise strategy or help the church initiate a three-pronged approach to the problem. He will do well to rise above his own time orientation and recognize that no one point of view with regard to time orientation is correct in every situation.

Punctuality is another aspect of chronemics that communicates nonverbally. For most Americans, it is important to arrive at meetings and social gatherings on time or a bit early. Employers routinely dock workers who arrive late. Those who habitually arrive late for meetings or social engagements are perceived as lazy and unorganized. An exception is afforded to high-status individuals in American culture. For example, people expect to have to wait for a medical appointment. Richmond and McCroskey (2000) explain, "It is the rare person who would arrive late for a meeting with the President of the United States. However, the President might arrive late and no one would think anything about it" (p. 206).

KEY CONCEPTS

Nonverbal communication has greater and longer-lasting impact than messages sent with the verbal message system. That is why effective pastoral communicators recognize basic truths about the nonverbal message system. Nonverbals generally fall into one of seven categories, including

- Appearance
- Gestures and body movements
- Facial expressions and eye behavior
- Vocalics
- Space and territoriality
- Touch
- Time

The pastor who develops the ability to accurately send and receive both verbal and nonverbal messages finds the work of pastoral ministry is accomplished with much greater ease and effectiveness.

MEANINGS MANIA

Work Bank

  a. chronemics
  b. endomorphs
  c. kinesics
  d. emblems
  e. haptics

    f. artifacts
    g. oculesis
    h. vocalics
    i. nonverbal communication
    j. mesomorphs
    k. ectomorphs
    l. proxemics

Definitions

_____ 1. Rounded, oval body type
_____ 2. Communication other than written or spoken language
_____ 3. Fragile-looking physique
_____ 4. Triangular body shape
_____ 5. The study of movements
_____ 6. Includes jewelry, makeup, and cologne
_____ 7. Nonverbal cues that substitute for a word
_____ 8. The study of eye messages
_____ 9. Includes rate, pitch, and volume of the voice
_____ 10. The study of touch
_____ 11. Use of space such as in a home or office
_____ 12. Study of how time effects messages

UNLEASHING THE POWER
OF INTERPERSONAL COMMUNICATION

Select a partner and place your chairs back to back so that you can hear one another comfortably but cannot see or touch one another. In this position take three minutes each to describe your favorite book.

Next turn your chairs facing one another and continue the conversation with three minutes each describing your favorite athletic event or hobby.

Finally, without speaking pan mime for your partner the title of your favorite movie.

Which means of communication is most comfortable? Which is most effective? What other things did this experiment demonstrate about the role of verbal and nonverbal communication?

Chapter 7

Listening

If ever a man needed the assistance of a wise and caring pastor, it was the best-known citizen of Uz, a man by the name of Job. In the beginning of the book that bears his name, Job apparently has no needs at all. He was a devoutly religious man. In addition, Job was a great family man. He and his wife's ten adult children include seven sons and three daughters. The family was close, meeting frequently together for dinner and family fellowship. Job's success also carried over to business matters. Among his holdings were, "seven thousand sheep, three thousand camels, five hundred yoke of oxen and five hundred donkeys, and [he] had a large number of servants" (Job 1:3).

But one day all the evidences of Job's success vanished in the twinkling of an eye. Hostile neighbors stole all his oxen and donkeys, fire fell from heaven and destroyed his sheep, raiding parties carried off the camels, and vicious winds destroyed the lives of all of his sons and daughters in one-fell swoop.

Three friends Eliphaz, Bildad, and Zophar rushed to Job's aid. They attempted to offer comfort and encouragement. As time passed, they continued their counseling relationship with Job in an effort to help him deal with the sharp blows of real life. In effect, Eliphaz, Bildad, and Zophar teamed up to become Job's pastor.

In their pastoral role the three philosophized over life, theorized about Job's losses, and urged spiritual renewal in the midst of what they saw as Job's obvious sin. But Job repeatedly rejected their counsel and insisted that his relationship with God was proper and holy.

Ultimately it was a pastoral tirade by Zophar that became more than Job could handle. In response to Zophar's words, Job appealed, "Listen carefully to my words; let this be the consolation you give me" (Job 21:2). One can envision Zophar beginning to respond, but Job continued, "clap your hand over your mouth" (Job 21:5).

A valid paraphrase of Job's response is, "Be quiet and listen. Let that be your ministry." Many modern-day parishioners have repeated Job's sentiments concerning their own pastors. "The first failure of many ministers, teachers, and others who endeavor to be people helpers is failing to listen" (Hatcher, 1986, p. 18).

Though Drakeford (1982) writes to a general audience, he too singles out pastors concerning the importance of listening. He writes,

> The pastor frequently sees his church work as expressive communication—preaching or giving devotional talks to civic clubs—and fails to realize that many modern-day people long for his listening ear. In fact, the majority of his church members would be delighted if their pastor would organize his time to provide for the vital ministry of listening. (p. 14)

Apparently Zophar is not the last pastor with the need to develop a ministry of listening. Pastor Kim seems to have joined the Zophar conspiracy in Pastoral Conversation 7.1.

Pastoral Conversation 7.1

Background

The Staff Parish Committee at Calvary Church is charged with the responsibility of conducting an annual evaluation of Pastor Kim, and submitting it to appropriate denominational officials. The committee has been involved in the process for nearly an hour. Thus far nearly all of the comments have been extremely positive about Pastor Kim's work.

Dialogue

CHAIR: According to the instructions we must include comments under the category "needs improvement." Who will begin the process for us?

JASON: I have one. I just hope I can say it correctly. Sometimes Pastor Kim seems just too busy.

CHAIR: I thought we had listed that as a positive, when we said that Pastor Kim has a good work ethic.

JASON: That is true. But the area that needs work is that Pastor Kim is so deep in thought she sometimes walks right by people and doesn't even notice their presence.

PASTOR KIM: (defensively) When have I ever overlooked someone?

JASON: Pastor, it's not just one time. It happens very regularly. People don't believe they are heard. They sometimes feel ignored. Frankly, Pastor Kim, what needs work is your willingness to listen.

Analysis

1. How should Pastor Kim respond to Jason's comment? Is there an effective way to evaluate the charge of poor listening?
2. If Pastor Kim becomes convinced that Jason is right, what can she do? Can better listening be developed? If so, in what way?

Undoubtedly, Pastor Kim will initially believe that Jason's comments are inaccurate. As with most people, she will probably overrate her own listening abilities. "Unfortunately, most of us think of ourselves as better listeners than we really are" (Nichols, 1995, p. 11).

Research indicates that most people remember only about half of what was said for a full day. After forty-eight hours, 50 percent of the remainder has been lost. In other words, only about 25 percent of the content of a lecture or speech is retained for more than two days. And, "our listening deteriorates not only when we listen to speeches or lectures, but when we interact interpersonally" (Beebe, Beebe, and Ivy, 2001, p. 125).

Most people are not nearly as good at listening as their self-perception would indicate. In the case of pastors, failing to listen can mean a failure to minister effectively. The Pastor's Listening Survey, Exhibit 7.1, is designed to measure listening effectiveness. Honest answers to each of the ten items on the survey will assist in developing an accurate assessment of listening skills.

A "yes" answer to three or more of the questions in the survey indicates some listening deficiency. Responding "yes" to more than five of the questions usually indicates the presence of friends or parishioners who, similar to Job, are screaming, "Be quiet and listen. Let that be your ministry." High-scoring pastors are part of the ever-growing Zophar conspiracy.

EXHIBIT 7.1. Pastor's Listening Survey

1. As people talk to you do you frequently think about other things?

2. Do you believe it is more important to listen for facts than for ideas?

3. Do you frequently hear every word a person says but not get his or her point?

4. Do you frequently interrupt to ask questions in order to clarify another's point?

5. Can you tell by people's words, phrases, and expressions whether they have anything worthwhile to say?

6. Can you tell by people's appearance whether they have anything worthwhile to say?

7. When you listen to someone do you frequently notice distracting noises?

8. Do you frequently nod your head or say "uh-huh" in order to make someone believe you are listening?

9. Are there certain subjects you would rather not hear about?

10. Do you believe that verbal skills are the most important quality for any leader?

STUMBLING BLOCKS TO LISTENING

Pastors often fail to listen as well as they might because they stumble over one or more of five stumbling blocks to listening. These stumbling blocks are noise, time demands, interruptions, focusing on facts, and hearing difficulties.

Noise

Arguably the most significant stumbling block to effective listening is noise. Noise is anything that distracts a receiver, thus preventing effective listening. Noise may take one of two forms. On the one hand, there is that external noise that acts upon a communication event making listening difficult. In addition, often the noise within a listener, internal noise, minimizes listening ability.

External noise may come from playing a television or stereo which usually averages about seventy decibels. Or noise may be in excess of fifty decibels if it comes from the sound of car traffic through an office window. Pastor Jerry found it difficult to participate in the meeting of the Education Committee while the church janitor ran the vacuum cleaner, probably seventy or more decibels, in the adjacent fellowship hall.

In a more long-term situation, Pastor Lemar became a pastor after retiring from a career in industry. Many years of unprotected exposure to industrial noise, which may exceed 100 decibels, had made it difficult for him to carry on conversations in the normal range of approximately sixty decibels.

Cohen (1981) points out that noise can have an effect not only on hearing mechanisms, but other physical systems as well. The Supreme Court concured when it awarded compensation in 1981 for mental and emotional distress because of noise to residents around Los Angeles International Airport (Cohen, 1981, p. 49). Nor are smaller cities exempt. In 2001, the residents of Kokomo, Indiana, a community of about 47,000, were bothered by an unidentified noise. More than fifty residents reported that the low humming sound produced chronic headaches, night wakening, and fatigue. The source of the low-frequency hum that was inaudible to most people was nonetheless investigated (Kazavorich, 2001).

Not all noise comes from external sources. Internal noise may take the form of attitudes, beliefs, or values about the speaker or the topic of conversation. "Attitudes such as pride, prejudice, and defensiveness can cause us to turn a deaf ear to some people" (Hatcher, 1986, p. 18).

Preoccupation with a topic may cause a pastor to listen more intently. This phenomenon, sometimes called selective listening, amounts to considering all nonselected topics as noise. By contrast, *insulated listening* is the tendency to avoid certain topics altogether. Insulated listening serves to broaden the noise field by zeroing in on only the key subject.

Time Demands

A second stumbling block to effective pastoral listening grows out of the demanding schedules of many clergy. Listening is work that takes time. Yet, often listening is among those tasks that are left undone when the schedule becomes too busy to manage.

That was the case for Pastor Justin, who was returning home from a denominational meeting in another city. He stopped at a small regional hospital to visit with a man from his community that everyone knew as Hap. Hap was not a church member or attendee, but he and Pastor Justin had developed a good relationship, such that Pastor Justin believed Hap might be nearing a decision for Christ. Hap had been in the hospital for several days, but indications were that he was recovering nicely from a mild heart attack.

Pastor Justin spent a few brief minutes with Hap, prayed quickly, and excused himself. "I've gotta run, Hap," he said as he headed for the door. "I still have to finish preparation for the Bible study tonight at the church."

"Couldn't you just sit for a minute, Pastor Justin? We haven't had much chance to visit lately."

"We'll catch up when you get home, Hap. That should be only a few days now. See ya!!"

Pastor Justin sprinted to the car and drove the last twenty miles home. On the way he mentally began preparations for the Bible study. With just a bit of luck he could get things ready in time. However, Pastor Justin's wife, Kelly, met him at the door of their parsonage home. "I'm afraid I have bad news," she said. "The hospital just called. Your friend Hap died about ten minutes ago."

Obviously nothing Pastor Justin could do would allow him to go back and rearrange his priorities in order to make more time to listen to Hap in his final moments. Listening had not been at the top of his scheduled "to do" list. The results were an eternally lost opportunity.

Interruptions

Interrupting is a stumbling block to the most effective pastoral listening. Sometimes pastors interrupt those who speak to them simply as a result of discourtesy or from having developed bad habits. At other times, however, interrupting can be symptomatic of a much deeper and more serious problem. That is because a listener's self-image can become the reason for interruptions. Low self-image can negatively affect the way a pastor listens. The low self-esteem listener often dominates conversation, and appears on the surface to be very much in control, while at a deeper level harboring feelings of inadequacy.

A group of pastors gathered at a local coffee shop regularly to visit over breakfast. Others in the community referred to the group as the "I can top that" table. As with proverbial fisherman, no matter the story it seemed that every pastor at the table had a bigger tale to tell. Often the "I can top that" listener uses such braggadocio to camouflage feelings of inadequacy and inferiority.

One team of communication researchers referred to the phenomenon as *conversational narcissism* (Vangelisti, Knapp, and Daly, 1990). Adler and Towne (2003) prefer the term *stage hogging*. The concept is discussed more thoroughly in Chapter 8. Here it is sufficient to recognize that the stumbling block occurs because a listener feels the need to change the focus of conversation from speaker to self. Frequently an interruption is necessary to meet that need.

By contrast, Nichols notes that "genuine listening means suspending memory, desire, and judgment—and, for a few moments at least, existing for the other person" (Nichols, 1995, p. 64). Ironically, pastors who are called to live the life of a shepherd, existing for the sheep, have a particularly difficult time suspending personal needs to become genuine listeners.

Mulac et al. (1988) reported that there are additional reasons why people interrupt instead of listening. They discovered that men tend to interrupt more than women and for different reasons. Men's interruptions are most often about control. Women interrupt in order to agree or expand on the speaker's topic.

Focusing on Facts

The most effective listeners are those who gain the total meaning from a speaker's words. They accomplish this total-meaning type listening by hearing both verbal and nonverbal cues and by listening carefully to what a speaker omits. Often, however, in a misguided attempt to be a good listener, a pastor will attempt to gain as many factual details as possible, or clarify that details are accurate. This attention to detail may in fact become a liability to effective listening. Pastor Tony appears to be focusing on facts rather than engaging in total-meaning listening in Pastoral Conversation 7.2.

Pastoral Conversation 7.2

Background

Parishioner Mick has a clear understanding of orthodox Christianity, and has yielded his life to Christ. He is concerned about a lack of assurance of salvation in his life. He is in the midst of conversation about that concern with Pastor Tony.

Dialogue

MICK: So even though I just keep praying and praying, I really don't feel like God has heard me.

PASTOR TONY: You say you keep praying and praying. How often do you mean that you pray about the matter, Mick?

MICK: Well, it's not an everyday thing, but the feeling just keeps persisting that God hasn't heard. Just when I think I have a breakthrough, something happens. Like yesterday, when I read where Paul said, 'This is how we know we are in him. Whoever claims to live in him must walk as Jesus did.' I'm not sure . . .

PASTOR TONY: (interrupting) John said.

MICK: Pardon me?

PASTOR TONY: John said that, not Paul.

MICK: Oh. Right. Whatever.

Analysis

1. Would you characterize Pastor Tony as a good listener? Give reasons for your answer.
2. What would you advise Pastor Tony to do in order to improve both his counseling style and listening style?

Hearing Problems

Although hearing and listening are two separate processes, the latter is highly dependent upon the former. "Hearing is a physiological process by which we perceive changes in air pressure and turn them into electrochemical processes in the brain" (Roach and Wyatt, 1988,

p. 13). Hearing is primarily a function of the ear, which is divided into three parts: the outer ear, middle ear, and inner ear.

The visible portion of the ear and inward to the eardrum is called the outer ear. The purpose of the outer ear is to funnel changes in air pressure into the working portion of the ear.

Inside the middle ear is a small passage that serves to intensify signals and channel them on into the inner ear. This amplification process is accomplished by means of three small bones: the malleus, incus, and stapes. Movements in the outer bone are transmitted to the next and then to the next. In the final phase of the amplification process, the stapes sends the amplified signal on to the inner ear by means of an opening called the oval window.

In the inner ear, a fluid-filled organ called the cochlea converts the mechanical energy it receives into nerve impulses. These impulses are in turn sent along the auditory nerve to the brain. Figure 7.1 shows the parts of the ear involved in the hearing process.

Injury or disease can affect any of the parts of the ear, creating a hearing impairment. In addition, almost every adult suffers to some extent from presbycusis, a progressive hearing loss, which starts in the early twenties. Presbycusis exists in individuals who receive normal sensation to the cochlea, but who cannot properly process those sensations to the brain.

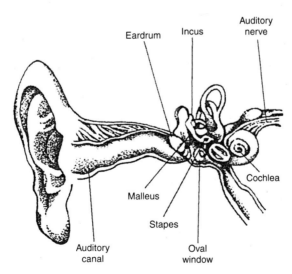

FIGURE 7.1. The Human Auditory System (Artwork by Tracy Thurman.)

The most common corrective device for persons with hearing loss is the hearing aid. Hearing aids have been improved greatly in the past few years. In addition, they have become an increasingly acceptable part of life for older Americans. Pastors experiencing difficulty in hearing clearly or in separating and sorting out sounds would be well advised to submit to a simple hearing test. An audiologist can determine what ranges are creating the greatest problems and prescribe the correct auditory assistance device.

Five stumbling blocks to listening include noise, time demands, interruptions, focusing on facts, and hearing difficulties. Pastors who strive to be effective listeners must do all in their power to avoid the stumbling blocks.

BUILDING BLOCKS TO LISTENING

Conversely, pastors improve listening by implementing five building blocks to more effective listening. These include

1. Utilize the entire listening process
2. Delay evaluation
3. Utilize the thought speed/speech speed differential
4. Listen with all the senses
5. Talk less

Utilize the Entire Listening Process

The opinions of communication experts vary with regard to the precise steps in the listening process. Adler and Towne (2003) see listening as a five-step process including hearing, attending, understanding, responding, and remembering. Beebe, Beebe, and Ivy (2001) view the listening process in a slightly different way. They suggest the important steps are selecting, attending, understanding, remembering, and responding. DeVito (2000) summarizes the listening process by noting the steps of receiving, understanding, remembering, evaluating, and responding.

All agree that listening includes at a minimum

1. Receiving
2. Attending
3. Attempting to understand

The specifics of the receiving process, discussed earlier, explain how it is possible for a listener to hear verbal messages. Not all messages are verbal, however. Hence, not all receiving involves the auditory process.

Pastor Lenny describes one of the most effective listeners in his congregation as a man who hears very little. As a result of a childhood illness the man has been left nearly totally deaf. He uses a variety of hearing aids and other auditory assistances. Still, when Pastor Lenny preaches, the man resorts to lipreading in order to gain anything at all from the message. "Often," Pastor Lenny reports, "he will ask a question for clarification as he leaves the sanctuary. He is one of the most effective listeners I have ever known."

One of the reasons Pastor Lenny's hearing-impaired parishioner is such an effective listener is that he pays careful attention. Paying attention and attending to important messages is crucial to the listening process. Americans experience a constant bombardment of audio-stimuli. Individuals who sit quietly for a full minute and list the sounds they are able to hear when they concentrate on the inputs around them will recognize that those same or similar audiostimuli are nearly always present. As a result, it is necessary to engage in a constant sorting out of which sounds to pay attention to. The selection process has tremendous impact on listening effectiveness. In short, many pastors listen poorly because they have subconsciously tuned out the messages they need to hear.

Pastor Kerry had become so accustomed to the complaining of the church secretary, Mrs. Ford, that without realizing it, he had effectively tuned out anything she said. Pastor Kerry realized the problem one day when Mrs. Ford related an important telephone message. He missed the message the first time and had to ask her to repeat it. "I'm sorry," he said with embarrassment. "I guess I wasn't listening." More precisely, the problem was the second step in the listening process, attending.

A listener who has heard and attended to a message has still only accomplished the beginning stages of listening. Parishioners give the highest listening marks to those listening pastors who listen most empathetically. Attempting to understand is an important part of the listening process.

Pastor Ray was engaged in family intervention with a teenager and his father. "He doesn't even listen to my point of view," the son lamented. "Of course I do," the father shot back. To prove his point, he repeated word-for-word all that the boy had spoken most recently during the session. That father had of course missed the point. He had heard words. He had paid attention to the words. But he had missed the message because he had made no attempt to understand his son's point of view.

Delay Evaluation

A second building block for the development of a more effective listening ministry involves delaying evaluation. From ATM (automatic teller machine) banking to high-speed Internet connections, culture is becoming increasingly instantaneous. Abilities in interpersonal communication are no exception.

In an attempt to keep things moving, many communicators begin the formulation of a response even before a speaker has finished his or her statement. The result is that often the later portions of a statement are lost or ignored.

Some listeners become so "good" at high-speed conversation that they can formulate a response on the basis of just one word. These words, sometimes called emotion-laden words, trigger a near reflex response. For example, for some pastors in evangelical traditions, the word "liberal" is all they need to hear in order to formulate an opinion about a speaker as well as that speaker's message. For their counterparts in mainline churches, the word "evangelical" or "fundamentalist" is enough to formulate a response about a colleague and his or her message.

Montgomery (1981) points out one danger of such short-circuiting of the communication process. He notes that for 500 very common words there are listed in the dictionary in excess of 14,000 definitions. As a result, responding to a single word out of context may miss the intended meaning of the word, let alone the message in which that word is used. The effective pastor delays evaluation in order to gain the entire message of a communicator instead of rushing to judgment.

Utilize Thought Speed/Speech Speed Differences

The average American speaks at a rate of 125 to 150 words per minute, but possesses the ability to think at nearly four times that rate (Wolvin and Coakley, 1996). This difference between thought speed and speech speed is one of the greatest liabilities to listening. The liability can best be understood by considering the thought speed/reading speed difference. Most readers discover that reading a textbook word-for-word provides ample time to think about matters other than the subject of the reading. The result is a lowering of reading comprehension as the mind wanders in an attempt to stay occupied.

Similarly, many listeners use the thought speed/speech speed differential for thinking about other topics, or simply for daydreaming. Effective listeners, however, use this differential to their advantage by summarizing the input, reading nonverbal cues, or considering what the speaker is omitting from the statement.

Researchers often study the thought speed/speech speed difference by using modern technology's ability to compress speech. In one interesting report on the effects of compressed speech, Weaver (1972) reported on a study by Emerson Foulke in which blind people were asked to report the rate of speech that gave them the greatest efficiency and comprehension in listening. The largest group, 45 percent, reported that 275 words per minute maximized the listening.

Listen with All of the Senses

Pastor Dale had preached a clear and convincing message on forgiveness. During the closing hymn, Pastor Dale noticed that a parishioner, Irene, was fighting back tears and glancing furtively about the sanctuary. Later Pastor Dale spoke to Irene about her reaction to the message. Irene revealed a deep-seated anger toward another member of the congregation who had wronged her. Pastor Dale was able to facilitate forgiveness and later reconciliation between the two because he had learned to listen with his eyes.

Montgomery (1981) declares, "The eyes have it," in the area of effective listening. He writes, "Rule 1, always look at the person you're talking to—and always look at the person who is talking to you. When the eyes are elsewhere, the mind is elsewhere" (p. 67).

Pastor Wayne, based upon his several years of experience in pastoral ministry, is convinced that touch is the most important sense to be employed in the listening process. He reports that when he visits a parishioner in the hospital, just offering an extended hand before the prayer communicates a great deal. Pastor Tyler in Pastoral Conversation 6.2 discovered a similar truth. People hear the concern of an entire congregation of believers through their sense of touch in that moment.

Drakeford (1982) lists touch and the eyes, along with intuition and head listening as components of what he terms whole-body listening. Effective pastoral communicators have learned to utilize all the senses of the body to best comprehend the sender's message. And, by contrast, pastors who limit themselves to hearing with the ears only are destined to be less than effective listeners.

Talk Less

Adler and Towne (2003) declare, "Most of us talk too much when we're claiming to understand others" (p. 284). Talking less does not necessarily mean complete silence. Clarifying the other's point or affirming a stated position may be very positive feedback and lead to effective listening. Talking less does, however, indicate not changing the subject as readily, not interrupting, and not stage-hogging.

Talking less may be a difficult goal to accomplish for those engaged in leadership through pastoral ministry because, "We think of people who talk well as leaders; we seldom credit leaders with the ability to listen" (Roach and Wyatt, 1988, p. 21). Instead, we view leaders as those who give speeches, offer sound bites, command others, or debate the opposition. In truth, however, all leaders are called upon to listen. Pastoral leaders have a special responsibility to effective listening.

KEY CONCEPTS

The five stumbling blocks that often prevent a pastor from listening effectively are:

1. Noise
2. Time demands
3. Interruptions
4. Focusing on facts
5. Hearing problems

As with Zophar of old, many pastors face these stumbling blocks to listening and never recover from the listening fall. Their Job-like parishioners cry out, "Be quiet and listen. Let that be your ministry."

But a growing number of pastors are discovering that effective listening enhances ministry. They are using the listening building blocks that include

1. Utilize the entire listening process
2. Delay evaluation
3. Utilize the thought speed/speech speed differential
4. Listen with all of the senses
5. Talk less

These enable a pastor to more effectively listen and thus enhance their interpersonal communication. As a result of effective listening these pastors more adequately meet the needs of their congregations.

MEANINGS MANIA

Word Bank

a. listening
b. conversational narcissism
c. cochlea
d. speech speed
e. insulated listening
f. hearing
g. inner ear
h. presbycusis
i. emotion-laden words
j. selective listening
k. noise
l. middle ear
m. thought speed
n. whole-body listening

Definitions

_____ 1. Preoccupation with a topic leading to more intense listening

_____ 2. Avoiding listening to certain topics

_____ 3. Converts mechanical energy to nerve impulses

_____ 4. Houses the cochlea

_____ 5. A small passage in the human ear that amplifies signals

_____ 6. A progressive hearing loss beginning in most people in their early twenties

_____ 7. 125 to 150 words per minute

_____ 8. Listening with all the senses

_____ 9. Anything that distracts a receiver thus preventing effective listening

_____ 10. 500 to 600 words per minute

_____ 11. A three-part process: receiving, attending to, attempting to understand

_____ 12. Shortcuts the listening process by triggering an emotional response

_____ 13. The body's process of changing air pressure into electro-chemical impulses

_____ 14. Consistently changing the topic of conversation to self

UNLEASHING THE POWER
OF INTERPERSONAL COMMUNICATION

Select an eight-hour block of time when you will be awake, and when this experiment will be least likely to interfere with school or work. During the period maintain absolute silence. You may want to carry a note explaining the experiment to those with whom you come in contact. Pay special attention to your frustrations, sensitivities, and heightened awareness. As a result of the experiment, contemplate how different your own interpersonal communication would be if you would talk less and listen more.

Chapter 8

Stages of Relational Development

Two fourth-grade students were engaged in conversation prior to Sunday school. "I'm having a problem with my mom," one of them exclaimed with a worried look.

"What's wrong?" asked the truly concerned playmate. "Are you and your mom having a fight about something?"

"Not exactly," came the explanation. "It's just that my mom is going through one of those stages where she thinks I'm going through a stage."

Truly, when one is ten years old, the stages of development can be a serious problem. Experts do believe that children develop in stages (Piaget, 1954). As a result, one of the common ways to study childhood development is to note the normative stages through which children pass on the way to adulthood (Meier et al., 1991). In addition, some suggest that developmental stages do not end with childhood, or even in adolescence. Levinson (1978) builds a strong case that adult males continue to pass through normative stages for their entire lifetime. His study provides compelling evidence suggesting that all human beings are "going through a stage."

GENERAL RELATIONAL STAGES

In a similar manner, communication experts have long maintained that decision-making and other task-oriented groups develop in identifiable stages. Tuckman (1965), a pioneer in the study of small-group communication, is perhaps best known for his four-stage approach to the study of groups. The Tuckman model integrates the task and social functions of groups, and suggests that groups typically pass through four stages of development. These are:

1. Forming
2. Norming
3. Storming
4. Performing

A similar model developed by Fisher (1974) is also descriptive of the nature of small-group development and communication. In his model, the emphasis is on interaction of participants and the systemic nature of groups. He labels the stages through which groups pass as:

1. Orientation
2. Conflict
3. Emergence
4. Reinforcement

Pastors will certainly benefit from a study of childhood development as they endeavor to work with the youngest participants in their congregations and their parents. In addition, an understanding of adult developmental stages would add to a pastor's self-awareness and also facilitate the encouragement of others. Still further, a careful study of the phases of small group development may be very useful to the pastor, who will invariably work with a variety of decision-making committees within the congregation.

But another stage model exists that may have even greater application in pastoral relationships—the model of stages through which interpersonal relationships pass in their development. Knapp (1978) is credited with having developed one of the best-known and most useful models of relational stages. He divided the rise and fall of relationships into ten stages that can in turn be roughly grouped into two broad categories, "coming together" and "coming apart." Knapp's work focused primarily on romantic relationships or very close friendships, but can be more generally applied to interpersonal relationships. He observed the stages of relationships as:

1. Coming Together
    • *Initiating.* This stage is very brief and marked by ritualistic communication such as, "How are you?"
    • *Experimenting.* The stage where communicators search for common interests.

- *Intensifying.* The "I" gives way to "we" as the relationship grows into this stage.
- *Integrating.* The two become one in the integrating stage. This stage is marked by the creation of a new person and the destruction of two former people.
- *Bonding.* Bonding is rarely achieved, since it is the deepest level of the interpersonal relationship.

2. Coming Apart
    - *Differentiating.* This first stage in the coming apart process is marked by a new emphasis on individuality.
    - *Circumscribing.* Communication declines in both quality and quantity since some topics are off-limits.
    - *Stagnating.* Relationships remain in this stage for long periods of time since it is often easier to stay together than to split up.
    - *Avoiding.* This stage is marked by distance both physically and conversationally.
    - *Terminating.* The ending phase requires a termination statement in order to redefine the relationship.

Relationships are not standard, nor are they predictable. "The ten-step model illustrates the range of possibilities, but it doesn't describe a guaranteed pathway for every relationship" (Adler and Towne, 2003, p. 331). Similarly, the development of relational stages through which pastoral relationships pass will have exceptions and limitations. Every pastor knows that life circumstances and personal interests allow for a deeper and closer relationship with some parishioners than with others. For example, Pastor Kerry had only been at St. John's Church for a few weeks when Howard Germann was killed in a tragic airplane crash. Pastor Kerry developed a much closer personal relationship with Howard's widow than with other members of the congregation as he shepherded her and her children through the grief process.

In addition, not every pastoral relationship even enters the coming apart phase of the model until a pastoral change forces a change in personal relationships. As a result, parishioners often feel as though no one can possibly take the place of their particular beloved pastor. When Pastor Cindy announced to the congregation that after a very successful six-year pastorate the Episcopal leader in her area was moving her to another congregation, the people of the church were nearly universally devastated. A series of short, less-than-successful pastorates followed. Others simply could not measure up to the idealized perceptions of Pastor Cindy.

In spite of the limitations, however, a general framework of pastoral relationship stages can be very useful. Such a model has five stages, including initial interaction, relationship building, relationship maintenance, relationship dissolution, and final interaction.

INITIAL INTERACTION

Even prior to the creation of a relationship there is a period of initial interaction. This stage is usually very brief, and may be marked by ritualistic behaviors. "Hi. How are you?" and "How's it going?" are examples of initial interaction ritual statements. Most people do not expect answers to the questions other than a ritualistic response. "Fine" is the culturally acceptable answer, regardless of life's circumstances.

The goal of a pastor at this stage should be to communicate openness to further contact, and to project that it is worthwhile for the other person to continue the conversation. During this stage physical appearance is very important since those qualities are most open to inspection. By word, posture, eye contact, and tone of voice a pastor communicates friendliness, warmth, availability, and openness.

The rituals of initial interaction reoccur at the point of every new interaction, even after a relationship has developed. In Pastoral Conversation 8.1, Pastor Kendall has failed to pass a test of initial interaction in one of these repeat beginnings with parishioner Gilbert.

Pastoral Conversation 8.1

Background

Gilbert is an elderly member of Pastor Kendal's small-town church. He approaches Pastor Kendall after morning worship, but his attention is obviously on a chance encounter in the local coffee shop during the previous week.

Dialogue

PASTOR KENDALL: Good morning, Gil.

GIL: Good morning, Pastor. I saw you at Molly's Café Wednesday morning.

PASTOR KENDALL: I remember seeing you, Gil.

GIL: I had wanted to introduce you to my brother who was with me. He doesn't go to church anywhere, and has a lot of problems in his life. I wish you would get to know him.

PASTOR KENDALL: I wish you had introduced us, Gil.

GIL: Well, I didn't want to bother you. You were obviously busy.

Upon reflection, Pastor Kendall recalled that he was pouring over his picks for the first round of the NCAA (National Collegiate Athletic Association) tournament while drinking his morning coffee. Because he had immediately looked down at his paper after greeting Gil, the latter had come to the wrong conclusion.

Analysis

1. Has Pastor Kendall done anything inappropriate? Has he done anything regrettable? Can a pastor be open to the initiating actions of everyone?
2. What should Pastor Kendall say in response to Gil's observation? How should he respond to Gil the next time he sees him on the street?
3. What, if any, action should Pastor Kendall take to make the acquaintance of Gil's brother?

RELATIONSHIP BUILDING

Once contact has been made or reestablished, communicators may choose to move forward in the relationship. Knapp (1978) likens the deepening stage to the sniffing instinct in a dog. Human beings tend to sniff around through small talk. Although busy pastors may see small talk as just a waste of time, in fact it serves several important purposes (Adler and Towne, 2003). These include

1. Uncovering topics of commonality for future discussion
2. Interviewing a potential candidate for a deeper friendship
3. Providing a forum for safe self-disclosure

As pastor and church enter the relationship-building stage they tend to be laid back and offer to one another a very low level of commitment. Perhaps that explains why most relationships in North American culture never progress beyond this stage. As Americans search for ways to avoid long-term commitments (Barna, 1990), one casualty is deep and meaningful relationships. When relationships do go deeper, however, changes in communication patterns occur that allow for more expression of appreciation for the individual and the relationship.

Pastor Glen reports that he was a bit taken aback and very pleased to receive an unusual call from a parishioner, Bob Bartleman, one Saturday evening. "Pastor," Bob said. "I just wanted to call and tell you how grateful I am for last Sunday's message and how anxious I am to hear your sermon tomorrow." Such encouragements, as any experienced pastor will attest, are few and far between. Part of the reason may be that such interactions typify a depth of relationship that few pastors ever achieve with their congregation.

One characteristic that indicates that a pastor/church relationship has reached this deeper level is that plural pronouns replace singular ones. That is, participants begin to see the relationship as "we" rather than "you" and "I." Notice the difference in two equally complimentary statements:

- "Pastor, I'm amazed at what you have been able to accomplish at this church in just the few short years since you came to be the pastor."
- "Pastor, I'm amazed at what we have been able to accomplish at our church in these last few years."

Although both statements acknowledge the pastor's accomplishments, the language of the latter statement also indicates a relationship that is fully formed and well accepted by the parishioner. Such a relationship has probably already moved to stage three—relationship maintenance.

RELATIONSHIP MAINTENANCE

Romantic relationships reach a stage where a new social unit emerges, distinct from its component individuals. Property, social spheres, and even personalities seem to fuse together (Knapp, 1978). People involved in such a relationship actually sacrifice some of the characteristics of themselves and become a new entity (Adler and Towne, 2003).

When such a phenomenon occurs in a pastoral relationship the pastor gives up some of the purely occupational characteristics that are associated with the pastoral role. That means, for example, instead of praying because that is the pastor's job, the prayer is offered because a friend is in need. A new sense of obligation to the church and individuals within the church grows during this stage. Both pastor and congregation have a high sense of expectation about the future and a high degree of fulfillment in the relationship.

In Knapp's (1978) final stage of coming together, *bonding,* there is a "public ritual that announces to the world that commitments have been formally contracted" (p. 21). Marriage is the ultimate bonding for intimate couples. Bonding is not just a ceremony, however. It also marks a change in the relationship. For example, in the marriage covenant, the "public display and declaration of exclusivity makes this a distinct stage in the relationship" (Adler and Towne, 2003, p. 329). The dyad now holds a new commitment to a common future.

That same commitment to a common future, or the lack of it, can be an issue in pastoral communication. As in the case of Pastor Leah who had trouble understanding why her congregation was so insistent that she live in the church-owned parsonage. Her husband's new job made it more convenient for the couple to move just fifteen miles to the county seat. She was willing to maintain strict office hours and was available to the members of the church by means of cell phone and pager. "In an emergency I can be here as quickly as most pastors would respond anyway," she pleaded with her pulpit committee. "You people know after five years together that I'll do my job no matter where I live."

"That's not the question," one committee member responded. "I certainly believe you will do your job. We just think the pastor ought to share in our community."

That is a strong statement of relational maintenance. In effect that parishioner declared that she or he wanted the neighborhood to belong to both pastor and people. The parishioner wanted to share all of the positives of her or his life with the pastor.

Although the issue was housing for Pastor Leah, the same concept often surrounds ministries involving a pastor and congregation who are in relational maintenance. Pastor Chris was extremely proud of the food pantry that he had led Ebeneezer Church in establishing soon after he became the pastor four years earlier. He was surprised, and more than a little hurt, when a parishioner asked in passing during a committee meeting, "Did we have that pantry going before you came, Pastor Chris, or is it newer than that?"

"They don't even appreciate my leadership," Pastor Chris wailed to a colleague. "She had no idea that the pantry was my idea."

"It sounds like a compliment to me," the older fellow-pastor corrected. "What she's saying is, 'We've taken ownership in that ministry along with you.' In the long run that means your work will persist long after you have moved on." In effect that wise counselor is advising that Pastor Chris's relationship with the committee member has entered into the relational maintenance stage. Pastor Chris may fail to recognize the stage because it is so rarely observed in pastor-parishioner relationships.

Pastoral relationships that are in the relational maintenance stage anticipate a long and productive relational life. Too often, however, frequent pastoral change circumvents relational maintenance. Congregations and pastors are actually afraid to enjoy the benefits of the relational maintenance stage. Such is the case in Pastoral Conversation 8.2.

Pastoral Conversation 8.2

Background

Pastor Rubin is part of a denominational system where pastors move on an average of every four to five years. He currently serves St. Matthews Church and has for the past two years. The following dialogue took place at a building committee meeting at the church.

Dialogue

ANNA: I'm just afraid this church is getting in over its head with this million-dollar addition.

DUTCH: But we have already been assured that we can take out a loan and spread the payments over twenty years.

CAROLYN: And that means that we can very easily handle the payments.

ANNA: Of course we can, the way things are going right now. But Pastor Rubin has already been here for two years. What happens when he is moved next year or the year after? We all know this church has had some lean years and weak leadership in the past.

Analysis

1. How would Anna's assessment be different if she had bonded with Pastor Rubin, or if she perceived that St. Matthews Church as a whole had bonded with him?
2. How should Pastor Rubin respond to Anna's concern?
3. In what ways do interpersonal stages compliment church growth research suggesting that longer pastorates produce more vibrant churches?

The attitude of Anna in Pastoral Conversation 8.2 is common among parishioners, especially where pastors have come and gone with frequency. Pastor Blevin recognized the need for relational maintenance and the common future that the stage represents. He used his knowledge of relational stages to convince the congregation to move forward. Under his leadership the church developed and approved a five-year plan that utilizes his skills in ministry. He thus initiated a common future between himself and the congregation's members.

As relationships with individuals deepen, the overall relationship with a congregation usually grows as well. Thus, between a pastor and parishioners there are numerous opportunities for deepening the relationship.

- Pastor Andy's relationship with the Wilson family quickly deepened within relational maintenance when he ministered on the

occasion of the death of their twelve-year-old son in a tragic ac-
cident.

- Pastor Laura's relationship with parishioner Bridgett deepened
  in relational maintenance as she helped Bridgett arrange for personal safety in the face of a domestic violence situation.
- Pastor Ross's relationship with Tyler, an elderly man in his congregation, deepened as the latter confided in Pastor Ross the
  fears and frustrations of caring for his ill wife.
- Pastor Chip developed a deeper maintenance relationship with a
  young parishioner named Brent as he helped the younger man
  sort out a call to ministry.

Each of these cases involved deep and intimate conversation where
thoughts and emotions were disclosed to a pastor who may well have
reciprocated the self-disclosure. Such is the nature of personal relational bonding. In most cases the depth of relationship with individuals leads to depth of relationship with a congregation as a whole.

RELATIONSHIP DISSOLUTION

Sometimes a pastor and a congregation must work through a relational dissolution. This process may be mutually agreeable, or may
be initiated by either pastor or the congregation. In other cases the
dissolution stage is entered because of problems in the relationship.
In still other situations, the timing is such that the best interest of both
pastor and people are served by moving on to new relationships.

Pastor Andrea reported that the long-range planning committee of
her congregation determined that they must envision a credible future
for the church without her. One member explained, "The life of this
church will go on when you move; so will our ministry." The statement may demonstrate a lack of satisfaction about a short-term pastorate. But, in a long-term and positive relationship such as Pastor
Andrea had enjoyed, the statement indicates that the congregation
may be entering a dissolution phase. Pastor Andrea would do well to
recognize the change in stages, look for other evidences, and prepare
herself, her family, and her church for change.

It should be noted that the person who spoke these words may be
not so much negative as wise. Part of Pastor Andrea's responsibility is
to help the congregation and its people prepare for her departure.

When her people can spiritually and organizationally survive without her leadership, she has done a magnificent job. Yet too often pastor's believe they must hang on to their authority and preserve relationships at all costs. Frequent moves lead to less-than-effective pastoral relationships, as does remaining in a local church setting where one's ministry is largely complete.

Knapp (1978) suggests several reasons why people linger in what he terms a stagnating relationship.

- To avoid whatever pain may be associated with terminating the relationship.
- To nurture a sense of hope that the relationship can be revived.
- To continue experiencing a perverse pleasure stemming from bringing the other pain.

One wise pastor quipped, "My goal is to move six months before the people in the church want me to."

Every interpersonal difficulty does not indicate that it is time for a pastor to move on. An individual relationship or two may come apart while a pastor has a growing, well-maintained relationship with the overall congregation. Pastor Mark and Darrel Barker in Pastoral Conversation 8.3 demonstrate all of the characteristics of just such a scenario.

Pastoral Conversation 8.3

Background

Pastor Mark and Darrel Barker have had several serious disagreements in the six months since Pastor Mark came to Community Church. In fact the pair have increasingly confined their conversation to small talk in order to avoid any sensitive topics. Darrel has missed the past three Sundays at church. The following dialogue took place when the pair met in the supermarket.

Dialogue

PASTOR MARK: Good morning, Darrel.
DARREL: Good morning, Pastor.

PASTOR MARK: We've been missing you the past few Sundays. I hope you haven't been sick.

DARREL: No, not exactly. I just decided to take a little break from Community Church.

PASTOR MARK: Oh?

DARREL: It's not like I've given up on God or anything. I've just been watching Grace Tabernacle on television.

PASTOR MARK: There's nothing like the fellowship of believers, though.

DARREL: So I've heard. And that is why I'll always remain a member at Community Church. But there is nothing like television preachers. You can always just shut them off if they develop obnoxious opinions.

Analysis

1. How should Pastor Mark respond to Darrel's last statement? What follow-up action should he take with Darrel?
2. Should Pastor Mark reveal this conversation to anyone else at the church? Explain your answer.
3. How would the situation be different if Darrel were attending another church in the community? Why?

FINAL INTERACTION

The ending of a relationship usually involves a termination statement. This statement signals the end of the relationship as it has previously existed, and indicates an expectation of what future interaction will be like (Knapp, 1978). Sometimes the statement is non-negotiable. Sometimes both parties to the termination give and take for some time in the development of the statement.

In Pastoral Conversation 8.3, if Darrel had announced his intention to join a neighboring congregation or said bluntly to Pastor Mark, "I'll not be back as long as you are the pastor," the relationship is certainly further along in the dissolution process. That statement would undoubtedly be at least a preliminary termination statement by Darrel. It may be his last word, or he may be open to negotiation with Pastor Mark about what the future relationship will be like.

Termination between Lillian and Pastor Dustin involved such a statement when Lillian said, "All the friends of my two teenagers attend the big church downtown. I guess for the benefit of my family I need to attend there with the kids. I hope you will still pray for us and that we can be friends."

In another termination statement a pastor heard, "I just have too much going on to continue in the men's accountability group. I'll still be as active as possible in other church functions."

Perhaps the most important termination for any pastor comes when it becomes time for a move to a different congregation. Here the emotions of termination are intensified because the pastor is simultaneously terminating with all the members of the congregation. Sometimes when relationships have been eroding, the termination comes as a relief to both the pastor and the laypeople. In other cases the termination comes as a shock to the laypeople of the parish while the pastor looks forward to the next chapter in ministry. On still other occasions, the congregation may vote to terminate its relationship with a pastor who feels the work has not yet been completed in that particular congregation.

The effective pastor will want to make clear summary statements that include a notice that he or she has no intention of crossing the ethical boundaries that forbid returning to perform pastoral ministry. This concern is explored more completely in Chapter 13.

FURTHER CONSIDERATIONS

Although an understanding of the stages through which a pastor's relationship with the church may pass is instructive, it does not tell the entire story. Understanding a series of further characteristics of pastor/church relational stages will prove helpful in building positive pastoral relationships.

The Process Is Cyclical

The stages of relational development describe many possibilities. However, most relationships do not move steadily through the relational development process in a linear fashion. Any relationship has its ups and downs. A relationship may develop as two pastors meet at a denominational convention and become acquainted. They quickly realize, however, that they have little in common and hold some vastly different theological understandings. For the remainder of the week they operate in the relational dissolution stage and by the end of the conference they are very willing to offer a termination statement and forego any future relationship.

Deeper Is Not Always Better

Many parishioners are very comfortable with a relationship with their pastor that remains in the relationship-building or low-level relationship maintenance stage. The pastor who tries to deepen every relationship in the church will not only quickly become burned out as a result of relational overload, but will ultimately achieve little more than frustration.

In an effort to become "good friends" with everyone in the church, Pastor Randy attempted to use his knowledge of relational stages to move every relationship with every parishioner to a deeper level. The effort backfired as people in the congregation began to see Pastor Randy as "coming on too strong."

Neither do relationships all develop through relational stages at the same rate. The rate is a function of the ongoing relationship and not the manipulative efforts, however well-intentioned, of either one of the participants.

Relationship Dissolution Is Not Inevitable

Relationships may reach a point of satisfaction for both pastor and people and simply remain at that level. No automatic property of pastor/congregation relationships suggests that unraveling is the inevitable norm. Relationships will entropy if there is no effort at relational maintenance. Pastors would do well to consider the advice of Canary and Stafford (1993), who suggest the emphasis should be on relational maintenance rather than relational stages. Too frequently pastors avoid the hard work of relational maintenance by simply moving on to another local church. One denominational official noted, "Many pastors who think they have ten years of experience really have two years of experience five times."

Relationships Are Dynamic

Conville (1991) declares that relationships are cyclical in that members of a dyad move through stages, but also return from time to time to stages they had previously encountered. This is also true of the relationship between a pastor and congregation. His analysis serves to remind the student of pastoral relationships that all relationships are in flux. There is no such thing as a static relationship. Either a relationship is growing deeper or it is moving toward the dissolution stage. As a result, the learning never stops for the student of relationships.

KEY CONCEPTS

Stages or phases of development help facilitate an understanding of how communication works. Experts have proposed stages for human development, decision-making groups, and general interpersonal relationships.

The unique relationship between pastor and congregation can also be better understood by exploring a five-stage development. The stages include

1. Initial interaction
2. Relationship building
3. Relationship maintenance
4. Relationship dissolution
5. Final interaction

MEANINGS MANIA

Word Bank

a. initial interaction
b. termination statement
c. relationship dissolution
d. final interaction
e. relationship building
f. relationship maintenance

Definitions

_____	1. The process of ending a relationship with an individual or congregation
_____	2. Heavily dependent upon physical appearance
_____	3. The "sniffing out" of another for a relationship
_____	4. Says what to expect of the relationship from now on
_____	5. Characterized by a growing deeper relationship
_____	6. Contains the termination statement

UNLEASHING THE POWER
OF INTERPERSONAL COMMUNICATION

Interview an experienced pastor about his or her last move, or consider the last time you were involved in a pastoral move. What were the circumstances surrounding the move? What evidences did the pastor see that it was time to move? What role did the congregation play? What role did ecclesiastical superiors play? What was included in the termination statement? How was the statement delivered? What role did the congregation have in formulating the statement?

Chapter 9

Power, Assertiveness, and Dominance

- Pastor Gil made a power play with the Administrative Board.
- Pastor Jennifer exerted her power over the committee.
- Pastor Anita is a power broker at the district level in her denomination.
- Pastor Joan powered her way through the Administrative Committee meeting.
- Pastor Carl's involvement in the citywide ministerial association put him in the midst of power politics.
- Pastor Renee overpowered all of the others involved in the discussion.
- Pastor Randy powerfully demanded his right to privacy at the Pulpit Committee meeting.
- Pastor Dave's problems at the church are reminiscent of the old adage, "power corrupts."

As these statements illustrate, more often than not the concept of power in interpersonal relationships has serious negative connotations. In fact, some find the subject of power in their own relationships to be so distasteful that they refuse to even discuss it. Wilmont and Hocker (2001) report that in one study of married couples, for example, participants freely talked about the subjects of persuasion, decision making, and handling of disagreements in the relationship. But questions about power caused these same couples to become much less open and free in conversation. Apparently they believed that power was so negative in a relationship that they refused to even acknowledge its existence.

This discomfort with power, or even a discussion about it, is especially prevalent in the church and with regard to pastoral relationships. Gula (1996) writes concerning power, "It is a hard reality for ministers to acknowledge because it evokes so many negative images: corruption, power-tripping, being one-up, coercing and exploiting the powerless to name a few" (p. 44).

One reason for this power taboo involves a widespread misconception of the incompatibility of power and ethics. May (1972) suggests a continuum on the use of power that helps to clarify the ethical issues. The left side of the continuum he labels *exploitative power.* This use of power dominates and controls another for the sole benefit of the powerful. A pastor who uses power in an exploitative way may use a parishioner for sexual gratification, or an entire congregation to boost his or her own ego needs.

May refers to the right side of the continuum as *integrative power.* An integrative use of power assumes equality with others and seeks to help them find their own strengths. One pastor declared, "The ideal church is one in which the pastor is gone for a few weeks and no one even notices." If such a church is to exist, it will be because the pastor has used available power to convince others to develop their own God-given talents and strengths for ministry.

The move away from exploitative power and toward integrative power is accomplished through avoiding what Brown (1976) refers to as "some unrighteousness tendencies of authority" (p. 139). He identifies four such tendencies, as follows:

1. Setting oneself above others;
2. Desiring to be served rather than to serve;
3. Drawing attention to oneself rather than the Lord; and
4. Expecting "head of the table" treatment.

The fact that some may fall prey to these unrighteous tendencies, however, says more about their personal inability to handle power than it does about the nature of power itself. In fact, power is an inherent part of all interpersonal relationships. Where there is human interaction, there is power. Wilmot and Hocker (2001) conclude that power does not reside in people, but between people. Power is a by-product of the relationship between the parties.

Thus, the wise pastor accepts the reality of power in relationships, while avoiding the "unrighteous tendencies." That pastor will seek to utilize power and authority judiciously. Such a posture grows out of a clear understanding of the nature and impact of power.

POWER

True power, the ability to influence the behavior of another individual, is in fact very important in pastoral relationships. A young pastor named Evan discovered very early in his ministry that he had tremendous power that he had not previously recognized. The discovery came as a result of a very brief conversation with a parishioner after worship one Sunday morning. That exchange is reported in Pastoral Conversation 9.1.

Pastoral Conversation 9.1

Background

Pastor Evan is a student pastor at a small rural church about twenty-five miles from the seminary campus where he enrolled just six weeks ago. He has just preached his second sermon ever. The title of this morning's message was, "The Nature of Heaven." Seated near the front of the church was Imogene Berrymore. Imogene is well into her eighties. She has been at the same church for nearly sixty years, and is a dedicated Christian who studies her Bible every day. She is considered the matriarch of the congregation.

Dialogue

PASTOR EVAN: Good morning, Imogene. It's nice to see you again.

IMOGENE: Thank you, Pastor. It's nice to see you, too. That was an interesting sermon.

PASTOR EVAN: Interesting in what way, Imogene?

IMOGENE: Well, I never thought about heaven like that. But, if you say that is how it will be, it must be right. I just need to adjust my thinking.

Analysis

1. Imogene assumes that what comes from the pastor's sermon is accurate. Is that a safe assumption? How would you suggest that Pastor Evan respond to Imogene?

2. If Pastor Evan has only known Imogene for a few weeks, how did he develop power so quickly?

Power Types

French and Raven (1968), pioneers in the study of power in relationships, have identified four typical types of power. These include

1. Legitimate power
2. Expert power
3. Referent power
4. Reward power

One explanation for the type of power exercised by Pastor Evan over Imogene is *legitimate power.* The term legitimate power does not imply that other types of power are illegitimate. Instead, legitimate power is the power that goes with a position or office. Legitimate power exists when a person believes that another person has the right to control his or her behavior because of the other's position.

For example, a police officer exercises legitimate power by holding up a hand to stop traffic. A course instructor uses legitimate power when she or he says to the class, "Take out a sheet of paper. We're going to have a quiz." In each case there is an assumption that the one in authority has the right to influence behavior because of his or her position.

Pastors have traditionally enjoyed a great deal of legitimate power in their relationships with others. In fact, DeVito (2000) notes accurately, "Teachers are often seen to have legitimate power and this is *doubly true for religious teachers*" (p. 246, emphasis added).

In more recent times, however, legitimate power seems to have eroded across many aspects of our culture. Pastors in particular have seen a systemic decay of their legitimate power, until many pastors today feel quite powerless. Harris (1977) maintains that, "for pastors, the sense of powerlessness is tied closely to the waning of the Church's influence in society" (p. 45).

Another possible explanation for Pastor Evan's influence over Imogene is termed *expert power.* Expert power is the power of knowledge. In as much as Imogene views Pastor Evan as an authority on spiritual matters including the nature of heaven, he holds expert power. Pastor Evan's expert power would be similar to a doctor's authority in medical matters or an attorney's power with regard to legal issues.

At one time pastors were among the few well-educated people in many communities. As a result they enjoyed expert power in many areas of life, especially in small towns and rural communities. Today, however, the general population has become more highly educated. Parishioners may view the pastor's expertise as limited to spiritual and ecclesiastical matters. In some cases laypeople have also become well-read in these specialized studies as well. Hence the reaction of Imogene to Pastor Evan's message is a modern rarity.

Effective pastors have, either consciously or subconsciously, substituted a third type of power for declining legitimate and expert power. *Referent power* is the power a communicator has over another when that other admires and wants to be similar to the communicator. Referent power may be termed the power of admiration. Thus, referent power increases as a person gains in popularity and admiration.

Pastor Paul made it a point to take time with and befriend young people. When one particular teen, Tim, developed some communication problems with his parents, it was Pastor Paul who was able to influence Tim positively. Tim admired Pastor Paul and wanted to please and emulate him. Pastor Paul held referent power over Tim.

Similarly, Pastor Jerry was very well liked among people at Garden City Church. The congregation found him to be personable and effective in ministry. Not withstanding, the majority were apprehensive about the financial condition of the church when Pastor Jerry asked for a sizable increase in salary. The raise was granted, however, as Pastor Jerry literally cashed in on some of his accumulated referent power.

One pastor spoke of referent power when he observed, "If the congregation likes you, you can do anything and it's okay. But if they don't, it doesn't matter what you do. It's wrong." His analysis is of course a bit oversimplified, but he did identify the impact of referent power. Likeability has enormous power.

A fourth type of power, *reward power,* is the power of those who have the ability to grant positive benefits to others. Positive benefits may include money, promotions, friendship, or attention. On the other hand, those who have the ability to remove positive benefits are said to hold negative reward power, sometimes called coercive power.

Pastor Mitch recognized his reward power in his relationship with Anna, the church secretary. Pastor Mitch was responsible for Anna's semiannual evaluation. In addition, he recommended her rate of pay to the finance committee each fall.

Pastor Mitch may not as readily recognize his reward power over Jim, a junior-high student from a troubled home. In the absence of any other positive male influence, Jim coveted Pastor Mitch's attention. As a result Pastor Mitch had the authority to impact Jim's behavior in a positive way. All Jim really wanted from Pastor Mitch was attention, yet any time a person wants something that another can offer, reward power comes into play.

Although the types of power that a pastor holds may vary from one situation to another, and even from one relationship to another, the fact remains that power is a factor in every interpersonal encounter. But where does the power come from? What are the sources that a pastor may draw on in order to increase power in pastoral relationships?

Power Sources

Gula (1996) writes specifically of pastoral power, and notes that power is derived from one of three primary sources. These include

1. Institutional power
2. Personal power
3. The power of symbolic representation

Institutional power is that power which comes from the ecclesiastical community. The act of being ordained, commissioned, licensed, appointed, or employed as a member of the clergy automatically carries certain powers along with it.

Pastor Barry convinced the administrative body of his church to support the regional evangelism thrust of the denomination. The fact that the larger body initiated the program gave Pastor Barry increased power in pushing for the adoption.

Similarly, Pastor Eileen was able to gain support for her stewardship proposal by suggesting, "Since the days of the Apostles, the church has called its members to tithe." Pastor Eileen's power was legitimated by the actions of the institutional church down through the centuries.

A second source of power, the personal source, comes from the fact that the pastor has gained abilities in ministry. Personal power grows with age and experience. As a pastor spends more time with a particular congregation his or her abilities become more widely known and accepted. This leads to an adjustment in personal power. Ministerial incompetence guarantees a lessening of personal power. This source of power is much more difficult for a young pastor to exercise. New pastors should gain a portfolio of pastoral successes.

Symbolic representation is a third power source for pastors. This influence is available to those who professionally represent God. "We are like everyone else in so many ways, but there is always something different about us. The difference is that we bring 'something more' to ministry than just ourselves" (Gula, 1996, p. 71). The "something more" may cause small children to identify their pastor as God, and adult Christians such as Imogene to accept their pastor's sermon as the word of the Lord. In effect, Imogene is saying in Pastoral Conversation 9.1 that she never thought of heaven in such a way, but God's representative has spoken. Therefore, in her mind, it must be so.

A fourth source of power is offered by Harris (1977) who believes, "The clergyperson's ability to acquire power to lead is interwoven with their ability to act autonomously" (p. 118). Such autonomy involves a pastor's inner confidence that he or she is not dependent upon the church, but possesses an ability to survive independent of the church.

Pastor Ross declared, "Ironically, I was never free to do ministry until after I had failed." The "failure" Pastor Ross referred to was in reality the experience of a very difficult pastorate. Pastor Ross had a vision for the church and what it could accomplish in the community, but the layleadership of the church did not share his vision. A great deal of division occured, which ultimately led to open warfare between Pastor Ross and the congregation. Later, in a new ministry setting, Pastor Ross felt liberated to be himself. He summed it up this way: "There is nothing they can do to me, or say about me, that I haven't already experienced." Pastor Ross was expressing emotional autonomy. He no longer felt captive to the whims of the church. His independence improved his effectiveness, and made him more powerful because he had gained autonomy.

Pastor Kayla's autonomy was more economic and grew out of a midlife career change. She described herself as "simply burned-out on ministry." Pastor Kayla went back to school, this time to a technical college where she earned an associates degree in dental hygiene. After several years in her new career she was eager to return to ministry. "This time," she reported, "I feel liberated because I know I can support my family without the generosity of the church." Pastor Kayla experienced new power in her relationship with the church. She is now in a position to use that newly acquired power in order to empower others to be more effective disciples of Jesus Christ.

Both Pastor Ross and Pastor Kayla have found the power of autonomy in their relationship with their congregations. They will need to exercise care that they utilize that power ethically and properly. One of the ways they can accomplish the proper use of power is to carefully note the differences between power and two closely related by-products of interpersonal relationships—assertiveness and dominance.

ASSERTIVENESS

Assertiveness is behavior that allows a person to exercise his or her own rights without diminishing the rights of another. The work of Cloud and Townsend (1992, 2003) wherein they maintain the importance of maintaining control of one's own life by insisting on boundaries has popularized the importance of assertiveness. Assertive individuals may also be powerful, but the two characteristics are mutually exclusive.

Assertiveness, and its role in interpersonal communication, is best understood by comparing it to two alternate types of behavior, *nonassertiveness* and *aggressiveness*. A nonassertive response is made when a person holds negative feelings inside. An aggressive respondent expresses those feelings, but in a way that diminishes the feelings of others. The assertive response avoids running roughshod over others, yet expresses feelings effectively.

When Pastor Clark received a call from Tyler Funeral Home it was clear that arrangements for a Friday funeral had already been finalized with the family of a man in the community. As a result the representative from Tyler said to Pastor Clark, "You are scheduled for the funeral at one o'clock in the afternoon, here at the home." Pastor Clark, who believed that Tyler should have requested his services, not assumed them, has three options by way of response.

1. *Nonassertive:* Pastor Clark can acknowledge the schedule and perform the service while seething internally that the people at Tyler have so little regard for his time.
2. *Aggressive:* Pastor Clark may respond in anger. "What gives you people the right to make demands on my time? Find someone who doesn't have anything else to do. And next time, call me in advance."
3. *Assertive:* Pastor Clark may respond, "Of course I'll do the service, under the circumstances, but I would appreciate it if the next time you would check my schedule in advance."

Clearly the assertive response is the only one that preserves the position and feelings of both Pastor Clark and the people at Tyler Funeral Home. "When you are assertive you still are taking the time to say what is bothering you but in a way that is controlled and nonthreatening" (Orr, 2002, p. 18).

Assertive responses are not just useful and important in negative situations. Even a compliment can lead to inappropriate nonassertive or aggressive reactions. For example, a parishioner said to Pastor Jose, "Pastor, that was one of the finest sermons I have ever heard." Pastor Jose may respond in the following nonassertive, aggressive, or assertive ways.

1. *Nonassertive:* Pastor Jose shrugs and mumbles with embarrassment, "Thanks. But it was really nothing special."
2. *Aggressive:* Pastor Jose declares, "It's obvious you haven't listened to near enough sermons, or else you have a terrible memory if you really think that was one of the best ever."
3. *Assertive:* Pastor Jose looks the one offering the compliment in the eye and says, "Thank you very much. I appreciate your kind evaluation."

Relational and personal benefits can be derived from appropriate assertiveness, yet many pastors choose nonassertive or aggressive responses. Emmons and Richardson (1981) attempt to explain why assertiveness is not more common. They note that "close-knit church communities produce a similar hesitancy to be assertive because of reluctance to hurt feelings or create discord" (p. 103).

Ironically, the greater discord comes unwittingly from pastors who allow themselves to be walked on by the whims of every member of the congregation. And the most likely aggressive responses come as a result of pent-up negative feelings that are ultimately released in inappropriate ways.

In practicing appropriate assertive responses, the pastor should be aware that nonverbal messages are at least as important as verbal ones. For example, using assertive language while looking at the floor in a nonassertive way will undoubtedly send the wrong message. Similarly, a harsh tone of voice can communicate aggression even when the words are more appropriately assertive. "In any situation of assertion, one should make certain that eye contact, voice quality and other components are expressed assertively" (Emmons and Richardson, 1981, p. 52). A more thorough examination of the effects of nonverbal communication is offered in Chapter 5.

DOMINANCE

Just as assertiveness is sometimes mistaken for power, so too is dominant behavior. Dominance refers to conversation control. Often communicators are assumed to be powerful, when in fact they simply dominate conversation. In reality, conversation control may have very little to do with who has power, and thus ultimately makes decisions that effect the behavior of others. One who dominates a conversation by talking the most, interrupting the most, and changing topics the most may also be the one who submits the most to the strong, albeit infrequently verbalized opinion of another (Palmer, 1989).

Pastor Deedra remained silent through the first forty-five minutes of Grace Church's important building committee meeting. Tempers flared. One group insisted on the repair of the old building. A second group just as strongly believed that it was time to tear down the old building and build a whole new structure. Since the two groups were nearly equal in strength a stalemate seemed eminent. "Remember our vision statement when you vote," was all Pastor Deedra said. The five-year plan of Grace Church mentioned a new building. The motion to build carried easily. Pastor Deedra had exercised tremendous power but had demonstrated very little dominance.

Examples abound of the opposite scenarios. Pastors can dominate conversation, but when the vote comes it is clear that they lack the power to seriously influence the outcome. Instead they have only exercised that conversational domination that has sometimes been labeled *conversational narcissism* (Vangelisti, Knapp, and Daly, 1990).

Conversational narcissism is the self-absorbed communication style in which communicators tend to talk glibly, confidently, and virtually uninterrupted about themselves and their interests. One way to measure the degree of conversational narcissism is to note the number of times personal pronouns are used in a conversation. Conversational narcissists are constantly trying to "one-up" someone in order to gain or retain control of a conversation.

> "You think you've had a bad day; let me tell you what mine has been like."
> "You think your congregation has great givers; you should see the stewardship report at my church."
> "That reminds me of an experience I had in seminary . . ."
> "The same thing happened to me a few years ago at a former church."

Most people shy away from such self-absorbed communicators, and choose instead to associate with those who engage in more appropriate conversational turn-taking. Effective conversationalists ask questions, listen, and respond appropriately. They may from time to time control conversation, but only in a way that satisfies both parties. Neither person feels ignored or unable to contribute. Such communicators are willing and able to pass back and forth the opportunity to speak. In addition, they allow conversations to develop by avoiding interruptions. These highly effective conversationalists may be less dominant than others, but ultimately, they tend toward stronger real power as a result of the more positive responses they generate in others.

KEY CONCEPTS

Power is the ability to influence the behavior of another. Types of power include legitimate, expert, referent, and reward. Pastors may derive their power from a combination of four sources. These include

1. institutional church
2. personal sources
3. symbolic representation
4. personal autonomy

Often assertiveness and dominance are mistaken for power. Assertiveness is any behavior that allows a person to exercise their own rights without diminishing the rights of another. Alternatives to assertive behavior are nonassertiveness or aggression.

Dominance refers to conversational control. A dominant individual talks more than others, but may not actually exercise power over others.

MEANINGS MANIA

Word Bank

a. assertiveness
b. dominance
c. expert power
d. institutional power
e. personal autonomy
f. aggressiveness
g. power
h. referent power
i. personal power
j. nonassertiveness
k. legitimate power
l. reward power
m. symbolic representation

Definitions

_____ 1. The control of a conversation
_____ 2. The ability to influence another's behavior
_____ 3. Exercises personal rights without diminishing the rights of another
_____ 4. Expresses feelings by diminishing another
_____ 5. The power of knowledge

_____ 6. Holding negative feelings inside

_____ 7. The type of power that is a product of admiration

_____ 8. The type of power that is a product of position

_____ 9. The type of power that comes from an ability to grant benefits

_____ 10. Source of power derived from personal abilities

_____ 11. Source of power available to the representative of God

_____ 12. Power that is derived from the organized church

_____ 13. Source of power that comes with the ability to stand alone emotionally or economically

UNLEASHING THE POWER
OF INTERPERSONAL COMMUNICATION

Arrange to attend the business meeting of a local church as an observer. Look for evidences of who has real power. Who is assertive? Who is dominant? In this setting how are the three similar? How are they different? Who appears to be the most powerful participant? Note how he or she exercises his or her power.

Chapter 10

Managing Conflict

To dwell above with saints we love,
Oh, won't that be glory?
But to dwell below with saints we know,
Now there's a different story!

Author Unknown

This whimsical verse might have been written by any number of experienced pastors. In fact, Pastor Ryan could have written it just after the dialogue revealed in Pastoral Conversation 10.1.

Pastoral Conversation 10.1

Situation

The monthly Administrative Council meeting of Community Church had just been adjourned with Pastor Ryan's closing prayer. The "amen" had hardly finished reverberating off the walls of the meeting room when Estel Whetmore rushed to a spot directly in front of Pastor Ryan. She had her hands on her hips and an angry look on her face.

Dialogue

ESTEL: What you have just done to this church is inexcusable. In the fifty-two years I've been attending Community Church there has never been such a display of disunity.

PASTOR RYAN: (with genuine surprise) I'm sorry, but I have no idea what you're talking about. What disunity?

ESTEL: I'm talking about what happened to Jake Adkins. That poor man had to stand all by himself in the midst of his grief.

PASTOR RYAN: You must mean his "no" vote on the motion to have the fellowship hall piano tuned.

ESTEL: That piano was given to this church in memory of Jake's dear departed wife. Rest her soul. His opinion ought to count for something.

PASTOR RYAN: Of course his opinion matters. But he was outvoted fourteen to one, not counting your abstention. And as to his grieving alone, Jake has been a widower for twenty-five years.

ESTEL: It is more than just the fact that no one seems to remember that the piano is in this church in the first place in honor of his wife. It is the idea that he had to vote "no." This church has always prided itself on its oneness. Now there is open conflict.

PASTOR RYAN: I hardly think a single dissenting vote could be classified as open conflict.

ESTEL: (turning to stomp away) Such disunity! And the pastor doesn't even seem to care.

Analysis

1. Is there conflict at Community Church? Explain your answer.
2. Should Pastor Ryan respond further to Estel? If so, what should he say?
3. Should Pastor Ryan take any follow-up action with Jake? Why or why not?

Estel and Pastor Ryan obviously disagree about the nature of disunity and conflict. That disagreement puts them in good company. Communication experts have also offered a variety of opinions as to the nature of conflict. Donohue and Kolt (1992) define conflict as, "a situation in which interdependent people express (manifest or latent) differences in satisfying their individual needs and interests, and they experience interference from each other in accomplishing these goals" (p. 4). Coser (1956) sees conflict as a "struggle over values and claims to scarce status, power, and resources in which the aims of the opponents are to neutralize, injure, or eliminate their rivals" (p. 8). Cross, Names, and Beck (1979) offer a much simpler definition. They see conflict as "differences between and among individuals" (p. v).

Those who examine conflict specifically in the church are no more unified in their understandings. McSwain and Treadwell (1989) offer their own definition of conflict when they write, "a situation in which two or more human beings desire goals which they perceive as being attainable by one or the other but not by both" (p. 25). And Lewis (1981) believes that "conflict is two or more objects aggressively trying to occupy the same space at the same time" (p. 73).

THE NATURE OF CONFLICT

With such widespread disagreement about conflict, one might reasonably ask, "Is there any common ground?" Several experts in interpersonal conflict note that even in the midst of this variety of understandings there exist several common elements (Wilmot and Hocker, 2001; Borisoff and Victor, 1989). They believe that the nature of conflict is such that in order to be classified as conflict an incident must include five important parameters. The five are:

1. Acknowledged struggle
2. Interpersonal connection
3. Select incompatibility
4. Interference
5. Scarcity of resources

Parameter 1: Acknowledged Struggle

A conflict exists only when two or more parties are aware of and acknowledge that a struggle exists. That acknowledgment need not necessarily be verbal. Avoiding the person, a silent dirty look, or a negative gesture may all acknowledge the existence of a dispute, but more than one party must know there is a problem before conflict truly exists.

Pastor Kim felt resentment at the way the Sunday school superintendent in her church recruited teachers. Pastor Kim believed she should have input into who would and would not teach. The superintendent saw recruitment as his responsibility alone. He occasionally gave the pastor an after-the-fact report, but never sought her input. On advice of a denominational leader, Pastor Kim said nothing about the matter to the superintendent. Instead she continued to boil on the inside. Pastor Kim has a problem. Technically this situation does not fit the definition of a conflict since the struggle remains latent but has never been acknowledged.

Parameter 2: Interpersonal Connection

In order for conflict to exist the two parties must be connected interpersonally. Although they may have deep antagonistic feelings, the parties in conflict usually need each other. They are interdependent.

Pastor Stephon feels strongly that the church has a major responsibility with regard to the couples it marries. As a result, he only agrees to marry those couples who are members of his congregation, and who agree to a series of premarital counseling sessions. Scores of unchurched couples in Pastor Stephon's community who soon plan to be married may take issue with his position. However, only the one couple that he recently refused to schedule are in conflict with Pastor Stephon. The others have neither an interpersonal relationship with him, nor an acknowledged struggle.

Parameter 3: Select Incompatibility

Those in conflict may have much in common, and even be working toward the same general goal. At some point, however, they have discovered and acknowledged an incompatibility on a select issue.

Pastor Tony and the chairperson of his church's evangelism committee agree that more people must be won to Christ. They agree that evangelism is the main purpose of the church. They disagree, however, about the process of evangelism. Pastor Tony believes that it is important to begin in the local neighborhood. He is, therefore, encouraging a door-to-door campaign for evangelism. The evangelism chairperson sees evangelism as best accomplished in mass meetings. The chairperson plans to use the committee's time and resources to support a community crusade and host a fall revival. The two are in conflict over the process and procedure although their overarching goals are identical.

Parameter 4: Interference

Even an acknowledged struggle, where people are connected inter-personally, and where incompatibility exists on some select issue, is not necessarily conflict without at least perceived interference. Inter-ference occurs when one person's behavior limits another person's opportunity to meet goals. No matter how different two people's goals, full-fledged conflict does not exist until one or the other acts in a way that hinders the counterpart from reaching goals.

In one church, conflict erupted over the time for the morning worship. For many years the church had changed morning worship from 10:00 a.m. to 9:00 a.m. when the country moved to daylight savings time in the spring. The congregation returned to the 10:00 hour when daylight savings came to an end. Pastor Kyle, however, believed that if the church were to be successful in recruiting new families, it would have to maintain a regular unchanging worship time. Although most of the congregation's participants were open to negotiation on the matter, Bruce McAlister angrily accused Pastor Kyle, saying, "If you're so interested in stability, why don't you leave things the way we've had them for the past twenty-five years?" Clearly Pastor Kyle's goal of church growth had brought him to a point of interference with Bruce's goal of avoiding change. The two are thus in genuine con-flict.

Parameter 5: Scarcity of Resources

Conflicts develop when people believe that there isn't enough of something to meet the needs of everyone. Money is an obvious scar-city that leads to many conflicts. At other times power, time, or au-thority can be the scarce resource.

Pastor Greg and Pastor Sean were members of the same denomina-tion who served churches in the same county seat town. The area was in serious population decline. The two came into a very serious con-flict when the outreach team from Pastor Sean's congregation began making Saturday evening phone calls at random to invite people in the community to worship the next morning. When one of the respon-dents told the caller she was an active participant in Pastor Greg's congregation, the caller responded by saying, "Many folks are switch-ing over. Let me tell you some of the reasons why." When Pastor Greg heard about the open proselytizing behavior he confronted Pastor Sean. The later admitted that members of the outreach team were trained to do exactly that. "With fewer and fewer people in the area," he justified the program, "only those churches taking bold actions will survive." The conflict between these two pastors erupted out of an unethical response to a perceived shortage of potential worshipers.

Even with these five parameters of conflict, it is sometimes very difficult to determine if true conflict exists. Every interpersonal disagreement is not properly labeled as conflict. One might reasonably ask, for example, if true conflict exists in Pastoral Conversation 10.2. Do all five parameters exist in the scenario?

Pastoral Conversation 10.2

Situation

Pastor Dale, late for a presurgery prayer at Memorial Hospital with Mrs. Owen, races up the hall and to the doorway of her room, just as an orderly pushes her toward the elevator.

Dialogue

PASTOR DALE: Thank goodness I made it. I'm sorry I'm late. I need to have a quick prayer with Mrs. Owen before you go.

ORDERLY: I'm sorry. The surgeon is waiting. We need to go now.

PASTOR DALE: (standing between the gurney and the elevator door) We'll only be a moment. It's very important. (Pastor Dale prays briefly with Mrs. Owen. He then turns to the waiting orderly.) Thank you for your patience.

ORDERLY: Yeah, whatever.

Pastor Dale quickly forgot the exchange as he went about his day's activity. A few days later the incident resurfaced. First, he heard from Mrs. Owen's daughter. She declared that her mother was very upset about the "rude way that he dealt with hospital staff." Later that same afternoon he received a letter from the hospital chaplain requesting an appointment to discuss a formal complaint filed by the orderly.

Analysis

1. Does conflict between Pastor Dale and the orderly exist? Is there conflict between Pastor Dale and Mrs. Owen? Analyze this situation using each of the five parameters of conflict.
2. How might Pastor Dale have better handled the situation? What should he do now?

CONSTRUCTIVE OR DESTRUCTIVE CONFLICT?

The incident described in Pastoral Conversation 10.2 has the potential to damage Pastor Dale's relationship with Mrs. Owen, the hospital orderly, and perhaps even the hospital administration, but is it also possible that the incident could have positive results? Usually conflict is thought of as a destroyer of interpersonal relationships because conflict is assumed to be negative and destructive. Simons (1972) noted a shift in thinking about conflict. Experts now generally agree that conflict is not automatically negative, nor should it be avoided at all costs. In fact, conflict may be of a positive nature that can lead to relational improvements in some circumstances.

Johnson (1997, p. 217) suggests four outcomes to look for in deciding whether a conflict has been constructive or destructive.

1. If the relationship is stronger when the conflict ends, the conflict has been constructive.
2. If the participants have increased trust for one another, the conflict has been constructive.
3. If both parties are satisfied with the results, then the conflict has been constructive.
4. If both parties have an improved ability to resolve future conflicts, then the conflict has been constructive.

Wilmot and Hocker (2001) agree that conflict can be constructive. They go so far as to suggest that sometimes conflict is best escalated to a point where it can be resolved positively. Pastors would be well advised to follow such advice with extreme caution. Intentionally agitating a situation in the hope of bringing about a positive outcome could have serious repercussions.

Donohue and Kolt (1992) note that time plays a tremendous role in whether a conflict participant sees the struggle as constructive or destructive. Obviously when in the midst of the battle, one may have difficulty identifying the ultimate constructive outcome. Later, however, people can look back and see that the conflict was actually very constructive.

Pastor Ryan declares, "There's no fight like a church fight." He lived through difficult conflict at St. Mark's Church over the issue of tithing. Key laypeople objected strenuously when Pastor Ryan preached on the importance of giving a tithe. Pastor Ryan held his ground through an intense struggle. Today he looks back on those early years at St. Mark's as foundational to a long and fruitful ministry at the church. Time demonstrated the positive results of the conflict.

CONFLICT MANAGEMENT STYLES

One key factor in determining whether the eventual outcome of a conflict is positive or negative is the conflict management style used by the participants. Kilman and Thomas (1975) discovered five common conflict management styles, which are generally accepted among researchers in the field of conflict management. The five styles are:

1. Avoiding
2. Accommodating
3. Competing
4. Compromising
5. Collaborating

Each of the five has advantages and disadvantages and may be applicable in a particular situation.

Avoiding

The avoider manages conflict with a very nonassertive and passive style, simply refusing to participate in the conflict. Johnson (1997) describes the avoiding style by using the descriptive illustration of a turtle that withdraws into its shell. Those who use the avoiding style usually have ample time to plan a strategy for the next step in the conflict development. They sometimes come across as apathetic. In addition, they frequently miss out on the benefits of constructive conflict. Often pastors who use the avoiding style spiritualize their approach by insisting that "turning the other cheek" is the only appropriate style for conflict resolution in every situation.

Pastor Danielle had trained herself to avoid the caustic comments about women in ministry that came from members of her congregation. Although she avoided the trap of a hot-tempered, off-handed response, she never allowed the latent conflict to escalate to the point where she could deal with it appropriately. When Pastor Danielle moved on a few years later, many in her church harbored the same untested resentments toward women in ministry that they held when she arrived on the scene.

Accommodating

The accommodating person puts personal needs and concerns aside in order to allow the other person to have his or her way. The advantages to this style of conflict management include a minimization of escalations. Hence, some conflicts are handled with relative ease. Disadvantages, however, are that the accommodator often harbors resentful feelings which ultimately damage the long-term relationship.

Pastor Herb was deeply embarrassed when he was asked by a grieving husband to leave the funeral home where he had come to pay respects. "You didn't care enough to visit her when she was alive," the man declared. "We don't need you now." It was true that Pastor Herb had made very infrequent calls at the woman's home during her lengthy terminal illness. A daughter had requested that he stay away, insisting that Herb's theological position on salvation and the afterlife had upset her mother terribly. By accommodating the daughter, Herb had missed a marvelous opportunity for ministry to the mother, and set the stage for his own embarrassing dismissal from a public place.

Competing

Those who use the competing style of conflict management frequently pursue their own concerns at the expense of others involved in the conflict. Competitors typically see only the possibility of win-lose outcomes and want to make sure they emerge victorious. The disadvantages of such a style are readily apparent. Advantages include the fact that the competing style can sometimes lead to very quick decisions. Competing, therefore, may prove useful in situations in which time is of the essence.

For example, when Pastor Adam was leading a growing church, a serious problem developed of providing enough parking for worshipers on Sunday morning. When an empty lot adjacent to the church was offered for sale, it seemed obvious to Pastor Adam and others on the board that the church should make a reasonable offer. Most believed that the church should act quickly in order to avoid losing the property to another buyer. Everett Hinton, however, sat on the church board. Everett was extremely conservative, especially in matters of finance. He suggested that the board consider the matter for a month and pray about it until the next meeting. Pastor Adam spoke against Everett's suggestion and insisted that the matter come to a vote. The meeting room was tense as Pastor Adam insisted that he win out over Everett's position. Ultimately, however, the competing strategy for managing the conflict ensured the church's long-term future. It proved to be an especially appropriate strategy in this case when time was of the essence.

Compromising

Compromisers are willing to give a little in order to gain a little. At first glance many believe that compromise is the superior way to deal with conflict in every case. Closer examination reveals that this strategy also has limitations. Compromisers utilize an intermediate style between accommodation and competition. Although supporters of compromise argue that everyone gains some in the compromise solution, everyone also loses some. Hence, as with every other style discussed thus far, compromising has limitations.

A small, one-room country church had an old metal roof that had developed some serious leaks. One group in the church believed that the metal roof was part of the aesthetic beauty of the building. Another group argued that a metal roof was outdated. "So long as we have to replace the roof anyway, let's shingle it," they said. The compromising pastor of that congregation saved the day when he suggested the left side from peak to eave be metal, and the right side be shingle. Surface harmony was restored as a result of the compromise, but the congregation became a laughingstock of indecision in the community, and their building a monument to the absurdity of some compromises.

Collaborating

Collaborating managers of interpersonal conflict combine a high regard for their goals with an equally high regard for the goals of the other. Pastors who use this style search for solutions that allow everyone to win. In fact, this approach to conflict management is sometimes referred to as the win-win approach. Collaborating depends upon a high level of trust between participants. It often requires a great deal of creative time to accomplish. Collaborators report, however, that the rewards far exceed the costs of collaboration.

When the traditionalists came face-to-face with the contemporary worship crowd at Pastor Dan's church, the resulting conflict threatened the very existence of the church. Collaborating, however, saved the day and expanded the church's ministry. An early service continued in a traditional worship style, while at 11:00 a.m. the more contemporary service was employed. Both groups obtained their objectives.

Collaboration also proved the appropriate solution to conflict between Pastor Aubrey and his church. Members of the Staff Parish Committee of the church believed it was essential for the pastor to live in the church-owned parsonage. Committee members were primarily concerned that the pastor would go to the county seat town fifteen miles away to purchase housing if they granted his request for a housing allowance. They wanted Pastor Aubrey to live in their community. Pastor Aubrey found the parsonage too small for his family and the layout did not meet the needs of his family's lifestyle. More important to Pastor Aubrey was the fact that the parsonage system did not allow him to build equity in a home. He recognized that at retirement time equity would be vitally important. When Pastor Aubrey and his Staff Parish Committee took the time to share their real motivations and interests, a collaborating position was not hard to find. The church rented out their parsonage and gave Pastor Aubrey a housing allowance. In exchange, he committed to seeking housing only in the local community. Both sides were happy without having to give up their important goals.

Clearly not one conflict management style matches the demands of every circumstance. Pastors do well to know each of the five styles along with the particular advantages and disadvantages of that style. To that end, Exhibit 10.1 summarizes the five conflict management styles along with their corresponding advantages and disadvantages.

EXHIBIT 10.1. Conflict Management Styles

Avoiding

Advantage	*Disadvantages*
Don't usually say things they later regret	Appears apathetic
	Ample time to plan strategy for the next step in conflict
	Miss the benefits of constructive conflict

Accommodating

Advantage	*Disadvantage*
Minimizes escalations in conflict	Resentment builds

Competing

Advantage	*Disadvantages*
Quick decisions	Someone has to lose in every conflict
	Escalation is common, especially when two competitors meet

Compromising

Advantage	*Disadvantages*
Every participant makes some gain	Every participant has some loss
	Some compromises lead to ridiculous conclusions

Collaborating

Advantage	*Disadvantages*
Everyone wins	High trust, creativity, and time required

NEGOTIATION STRATEGIES

The process of working through the issues of a conflict is known as negotiation. Collins (2005) points out that negotiation is a very common activity among managers and other professionals. She suggests "negotiation is an ongoing part of relationships" (p. 75). Yet, even those business managers who hold a master's of business administration (MBA) degree have arguably less than adequate training in conflict management (Reinsch and Shelby, 1999). Most pastors have little if any such training in the process of negotiation. Negotiation can be reduced to six simple steps. Utilizing the steps carefully helps overcome any training deficiency and leads to a positive relational outcome in the midst of even the most difficult conflicts. Effective pastors would do well to carefully implement this six-step approach to negotiation.

Step 1: Confrontation

Frequently pastors view conflict and confrontation as the same thing. They hesitate to confront, therefore, thinking that to do so is to stir up trouble. In fact, confrontation is the first and very necessary step to working though the conflict successfully. Confrontation is the expression of one's view of the conflict and one's feelings about it. Confrontation also encourages the other person to share his or her point of view on the matter. The act of confrontation says to another, "I care enough about our relationship to want to work through these difficulties." Confrontation must be done gently and lovingly if the pastor is to achieve the desired goals of clarifying the issues, defining needs, and admitting current feelings.

Step 2: Acknowledgment

Every story has two sides. A major step in successful conflict resolution is to acknowledge that the other's point of view exists and is viable. This does not mean accepting the other's goals and opinions to the exclusion of one's own. Instead, it means that the two parties carefully communicate to ensure understanding of the problem and the positions. The acknowledgment step will sometimes lead to immediate conflict resolution because as the two parties each clarify their position, they come to realize that their differences are more semantic than substantive.

Step 3: Agreement

In this step participants must search for points of agreement. They may find it beneficial to acknowledge once again the points of disagreement, but the agreements should be the emphasis. For example, a pastor may say in this step, "We may not agree yet on how to accomplish it, but we both want our church to be a good steward of its resources." Agreements become the basis for ongoing negotiation.

Step 4: Strategizing

Here the participants brainstorm together for suitable solutions while remembering that the best solution is one in which both participants win. At this point then, the search is for a win-win solution. The participants should not succumb to the temptation to save time by settling for a compromise if one is not necessary. Each potential solution should be carefully evaluated by both participants and compared to objective criteria in order to ensure a win-win approach (Fisher, Ury, and Patton, 1991).

Step 5: Implementation

In step five the participants attempt to implement their agreed-upon strategy for resolving the conflict. Some strategies do not work out as well as participants had hoped. In these cases it may be necessary to return to step 4 until a more workable strategy is developed. When the process has been effective, the conflict participants now have become partners in working out a solution.

Step 6: Evaluation

Those who were once combatants must revisit the conflict from time to time in order to evaluate the success of their implementation. In addition, the relationship itself should be evaluated in an effort to ensure that future conflicts can be handled in an appropriate manner. That should be relatively easy, since at this stage in the process the emphasis will be more on the relationship than on the once paramount conflict.

KEY CONCEPTS

Conflict is a universal part of interpersonal relationships, yet pastors often fail to properly recognize and deal with it. Conflict exists in a relationship any time five parameters come together. These parameters are:

1. Acknowledged struggle
2. Interpersonal connection
3. Select incompatibility
4. Interference
5. Scarcity of resources

In order to bring about the most positive outcome from a conflict, the pastor will need to choose the conflict management style that is right for the circumstances. Management style options include

1. Avoiding
2. Accommodating
3. Competing
4. Compromising
5. Collaborating

Usually, the collaborative style leads to a win-win outcome. Collaboration is not commonly employed, however, because of the tremendous amount of time required to resolve conflict by means of collaboration.

Negotiating a positive outcome to conflict is accomplished by means of a six-step process. The negotiation steps are:

1. Confrontation
2. Acknowledgement
3. Agreement
4. Strategizing
5. Implementation
6. Evaluation

MEANINGS MANIA

Word Bank

   a. conflict
   b. competing
   c. confrontation
   d. avoiding
   e. compromising
   f. negotiation
   g. accommodating
   h. collaborating
   i. strategizing
   j. implementation
   k. agreement
   l. evaluation
  m. acknowledgement

Definitions

_____ 1. Conflict management style that simply ignores the conflict
_____ 2. Give-and-take style of conflict management
_____ 3. The process of working through the issues of a conflict
_____ 4. The conflict management style that searches for a win-win solution
_____ 5. Allows the other to have his or her way as a conflict management style
_____ 6. Defined by the presence of a series of parameters
_____ 7. Expressing one's views about a conflict and inviting another to reciprocate
_____ 8. Pursuing one's own goals at the expense of the others as a conflict management style
_____ 9. Searching for the common ground in a conflict
_____ 10. Affirming the other's position
_____ 11. The search for a potential solution to the conflict
_____ 12. Going back over the conflict and its solution for the sake of the relationship
_____ 13. Putting the strategy for conflict resolution into place

UNLEASHING THE POWER
OF INTERPERSONAL COMMUNICATION

Consider a recent conflict situation that you have personally experienced. Be certain the situation you choose fits the true definition of conflict. Use the situation to respond to the following questions.

1. How was the conflict resolved?
2. How might it have been better resolved?
3. What pattern in your personal conflict resolution style is indicated?
4. How could your personal style have been improved?

Chapter 11

Forgiveness

The world watched in horror as a bullet thrust Pope John Paul II backward in his seat in St. Peter's Square. Even as John Paul recovered from his wounds, Mehmet Ali Agca was convicted of the attempted assassination. Not quite three years later Morrow (1984) reported, "Last week in an extraordinary moment of grace, the violence in St. Peter's Square was transformed. In a bare, white-walled cell in Rome's Rebibbia prison, John Paul tenderly held the hand that had held the gun that was meant to kill him" (p. 28). Morrow continued to describe how the Pope sat in the cell with Agca for more than twenty minutes as the two talked softly. Morrow writes, "The Pope forgave him for the shooting" (Morrow, 1984, p. 84).

Nearly ten years later another high-profile act of clergy forgiveness involved Chicago's Cardinal Joseph Bernardin. In 1993, Steven Cook accused Bernardin of having sexually abused him in the 1970s. Later, Cook admitted that his childhood memories were unreliable, dropped his ten-million dollar lawsuit, and sought the cardinal's forgiveness. In addition to his apology, however, Cook requested that the cardinal look him in the eye and declare his innocence. The cardinal offered the requested declaration, and then celebrated mass for Cook and a friend. Later, the cardinal, reflecting on the forgiving experience, commented, "I think I have grown spiritually as a result of this" (Woodward, 1995, p. 62).

Yet another incident of highly publicized clergy forgiveness occurred late in 1985. Father Lawrence Martin Jenco, along with Terry Anderson and Thomas Sutherland, had been hostages of Shiite Muslims in Lebanon. For months Jenco was deprived of fresh air, a bath, and medical attention for a painful eye infection. His captivity included severe beatings and long-term confinements in a three-by-six-foot closet. Jenco (1995) recalls the request of one of his captors for forgiveness on the day of his release. "As I sat blindfolded, unable to see the man who had been my enemy, I understood I was called to forgive, to let go of revenge, retaliation, and vindictiveness. And I was challenged to forgive him unconditionally . . . I understood I was to say yes" (p. 14).

Most members of the clergy will not be called upon to forgive in such high-profile circumstances as Pope John Paul, Cardinal Bernardin, or Father Jenco. Pastors do suffer emotional pain, public humiliation, and personal insult at the hands of members of their own flock. Forgiveness is an important aspect of pastoral interpersonal relationships.

Edward (1994) asks, "Have there been many others who have been mistreated so severely? Yes, mistreated, abused—so severely that it amounts to a crucifixion" (p. 12). Some may argue that equating pastoral mistreatment with crucifixion is a bit overdramatic. Few experienced pastors would argue against the notion that the circumstances of pastoral ministry are such that clergy must learn to forgive.

McKeever (2001) describes a scenario that later called for pastoral forgiveness. Church leaders, dissatisfied because their pastor had a different set of skills from those of his long-tenured predecessor, paid a visit to the parsonage. They threatened, "You need to be making plans to leave. If you leave quietly, there'll be no trouble. If you don't, there will be a public move to have you fired" (McKeever, 2001, p. 60). How does one respond to the clear call of God to forgive in the wake of such unjust treatment? That is precisely the question facing a pastor and his wife in Pastoral Conversation 11.1.

Pastoral Conversation 11.1

Background

Pastor Mitch and his wife, Camie, are looking through the morning mail. In the stack is a letter from a former pastorate, the Church of the Good Shepherd. The letter invites them to come join in the festivities of the church's annual homecoming.

Dialogue

CAMIE: Well look at that! Inviting us like old friends. It takes real nerve to think they can behave as if nothing ever happened.

PASTOR MITCH: Well, it has been nearly two years. They say time heals all wounds. Maybe the people at the Church of the Good Shepherd are counting on it.

CAMIE: While they're counting, they can count me out. I don't care if I ever see them or that place again.

PASTOR MITCH: Maybe it's time to forgive.

CAMIE: Mitch, I can't believe you would even consider accepting that invitation after the way they treated you. It wasn't enough that they fired you without any cause, but to add insult to injury, they refused to give you your last month's pay.

PASTOR MITCH: It still hurts when I think of that last board meeting when I ask, "Why?"

CAMIE: Do you remember their answer? They said the only reason was because you would benefit spiritually from suffering.

PASTOR MITCH: Oh I remember, Camie. But I also remember that scripture calls us to forgive. It's just that in this case I'm not sure how to go about it.

Analysis

1. Should Pastor Mitch and Camie return to the Church of the Good Shepherd for homecoming? Defend your response.
2. How would you advise them with regard to forgiveness in this situation?
3. Are there limits to a pastor's capacity to forgive? Are there limits on the Bible's command to forgive? How do those limits impact this situation?

FORGIVENESS MYTHS

Many pastors find it difficult to forgive. One reason lies in the fact that despite seminary training and many years of pastoral experience, pastors may have a faulty understanding of forgiveness. Several popular myths about forgiveness persist.

Myth 1: Forgiving Is Forgetting

The proverbial expression, "forgive and forget," sounds pious, but in reality it perpetuates a false notion about the nature of forgiveness. Many believe that since they lack the ability to remove past injustices from their consciousness, they also lack the capacity to forgive. In fact, forgiving and forgetting involve separate and distinct activities. There is no Biblical command to develop spiritual amnesia.

Pastor Al had been hurt when a parishioner declared at an Outreach Committee meeting that his sermons were weak. "That's the reason our church isn't growing," she declared. "People just don't get fed when they worship here." Pastor Al believed the comments were inaccurate and even irrelevant. "The purpose of worship," he fumed to his wife, "is God-centered, not people-centered. Even if people don't 'get fed,' what has that to do with worship?" As time passed, the sting of the comment subsided. Still Pastor Al found himself recalling the event whenever he saw that particular parishioner. "I'm a spiritual failure," he lamented. "I've not been able to forgive her after all these months. I'm reminded of her words every time I see her." Pastor Al had equated forgiving with forgetting. As a result he has become bogged down with regard to the clear command of scripture to forgive.

Gwinn (2001) correctly notes that the difficult and emotional experiences of life we may never forget. The God who created human beings is aware of their memory capabilities, which is why Jesus' command to forgive is not a command to forget.

Imagine how much different Pastor Al's outlook would be if he recognized this important distinction. Now every time he sees the particular offending parishioner he takes the remembrance as yet another opportunity to consciously forgive. His recollection might prompt the prayer, "Lord, thank you for reminding me that I have forgiven Mrs. Jones. Please help me to deal with the pain of remembering."

Myth 2: Forgiving Is Reconciling

What Pastor Mitch and Camie must decide in Pastoral Conversation 11.1 is whether they will reconcile with the Church of the Good Shepherd. They are commanded in scripture to forgive. Reconciliation is an option that may or may not follow.

Writing from a psychological perspective, Witvliet (2001) points out that forgiveness and reconciliation are best thought of as cousins, not twins. She further notes that sometimes the perpetrator has died or lost contact with the forgiver, making reconciliation impossible. This does not minimize the need for forgiveness.

Seamands' (1995) understanding of the difference between forgiveness and reconciliation grows out of his pastoral counseling experiences in abusive domestic situations. As a result, in many of his counseling scenarios, reconciliation may be inappropriate, even dangerous. He further suggests that reconciliation is a two-way street, while forgiveness can be one-way. God commands forgiveness, realizing that any of His children can fulfill that command alone. If reconciliation were the requirement, many would be forced to disobedience because the other person involved in the altercation refused to be reconciled.

Myth 3: Forgiving Is Minimizing the Offense

Pastor Grant knew he had done wrong and felt terribly guilty. Judy, the choir director at his church, had asked about scheduling the annual "Focus on Praise" Sunday, which featured the choir and an extended time of praise and worship. The problem came when she had inquired just as he was about to open the door to the platform to lead the choir into position for morning worship. "If only I had said calmly, 'Let's look at the calendar together right after worship,'" he lamented. Instead, Pastor Grant had exploded inappropriately about having to do everything and the need for leaders in this church to grow up. Pastor Grant had apologized immediately after the worship service and genuinely sought Judy's forgiveness. Her response, "It was nothing," did little to assuage his guilt. His behavior had been significantly inappropriate, and Pastor Grant knew it.

"One thing that doesn't help is to lie about the wrong. It's no good saying 'Oh, it wasn't really all that big a deal. I shouldn't have gotten so upset'" (Countryman, 1998, p. 49). In fact, true forgiveness always begins with an accurate assessment of the wrong.

Myth 4: Forgiving Is Taking the Blame

A similar myth assumes that forgiveness is the same as taking or sharing the blame. The notion that it takes two to fight, and therefore, two are always responsible for interpersonal wrongs, fuels this myth. In response to requests for forgiveness, people sometimes respond with phrases such as:

> "I'm sure I was wrong, too."
> "We both were upset."
> "I was as much to blame as you."
> "It takes two to fight."
> "No really, it's my fault."

These may or may not be accurate assessments of a conflict. They are never statements of forgiveness.

Had Judy responded to Pastor Mitch's plea for forgiveness with, "It was as much my fault as yours," she would have probably been making an accurate assessment. In reality, Judy probably did contribute to Pastor Mitch's outburst as a result of her inappropriate timing. Yet, sharing the blame is not what Pastor Mitch seeks or needs. "It was as much my fault as yours. I forgive you for the outburst. Will you forgive me for my very poor timing?" is a much more comprehensive statement of forgiveness. Such a statement serves to benefit both Pastor Mitch as the perpetrator and Judy as the forgiver.

Myth 5: Forgiving Is Perpetuating Injustice

Often pastors refuse to forgive because they are convinced that they were right. To forgive, they reason, would make it appear that wrong is triumphing over right. For example, Pastor Rob had been deeply hurt by the biting comment of Iris Doore, a member of his pulpit committee. During the annual pastoral evaluation Iris had commented in the committee meeting, "I don't know why we have to go through this evaluation stuff every year. It doesn't make any difference anyway. The pastor just keeps doing whatever he wants to do." Pastor Rob was especially hurt by the comment since he took the annual evaluation very seriously and made attempts on the basis of the committee's input to improve his performance. When a note of apology arrived in the mail from Iris, Pastor Rob's response was swift and negative. "She lies about me and embarrasses me in public, and then asks forgiveness in a private letter. She hasn't learned her lesson and if I make it too easy on her she never will."

The truth is that rather than perpetuating injustice, forgiveness breaks the cycle of injustice. Augsburger (1981) said it well when he wrote, "Wrongdoing is not a valid reason for my refusing to value and love another" (p. 60). Or as one pastor put it, "Two wrongs never made anything right."

A pastor may occasionally discover that deciding to forgive does only lead to more evil and offense. Some do indeed receive forgiveness as a green light for additional misdeed. Peter was speaking for many church leaders when he asked incredulously, "How many times shall I forgive my brother when he sins against me? Up to seven times?" Jesus' response, "I tell you, not seven times, but seventy-times-seven," (Matthew 18:21-22), was designed to help Peter see that life is not about keeping score. The phrase "seventy times seven" is indication of the importance of developing a habit of forgiveness. About Jesus' answer, Countryman (1998) notes, "Forgiveness, then, isn't just a series of actions, it's a way of life. It is as if Jesus said, 'Just make a habit of it'" (p. 117). That is good advice for church leaders whether in the first century or more modern times.

Myth 6: Forgiving Is Unimportant

Many pastors believe that forgiveness is not worth the effort. "Since forgiveness is so difficult, why bother?" they ask. The question, "Why forgive?" has several answers.

Forgiveness Improves Spiritual Well-Being

The clear command of God in scripture is to forgive. As with other spiritual disciplines, obeying the command may not be easy, but forgiveness is an act of spiritual obedience. Countryman (1998) relates the spiritual benefit to his responsibility as a teacher. He believes that when he teaches he repays a debt that he owes to all of those who have taught him through the years. Similarly, every believer owes a debt of forgiveness to Jesus Christ. To forgive is to begin the repayment of that debt. Sande (2004) lists "glorify God" as the first of four Gs of resolving conflict. He thus demonstrates the spiritual dimension of appropriate forgiveness.

Forgiveness Improves Emotional Well-Being

McCullough, Sandage, and Worthington (1997) point out that forgiveness has mental health benefits. Genuine forgiveness leads to a greater sense of personal power and life satisfaction. Higher levels of forgiveness have been associated with higher self-esteem, and better overall mental health. Freedman and Enright (1996) found that to be true in their study using victims of incest. So too did Coyle and Enright (1997), whose subjects were men who expressed hurt over their partners' decision for abortion. This combined evidence makes a strong case for the notion that forgiveness leads to improved emotional well-being.

Forgiveness Improves Physical Well-Being

About forgiveness, Michaud (1999) writes, "It's the hottest new medically proven lifesaver" (p. 110). Althogh the developers of empirical data may not share Michaud's enthusiasm, a growing body of evidence suggests a correlation between forgiveness and physical health (Cool, 2004). Witvliet, Ludwig, and Vander Laan (2001) demonstrated that forgiving leads to improved heart rate and blood pressure. In a similar study, Huang and Enright (2000) found the positive effects of forgiveness on blood pressure were greater when the forgiving was done voluntarily rather than from a sense of obligation. "The experimental research suggests that forgiving and unforgiving responses could have long-term effects on health if they are sufficiently frequent, intense, and enduring" (Witvliet, 2001, p. 218).

Forgiveness Improves Pastoral Effectiveness

As teachers of the faith, pastors have an even greater responsibility to forgive than other Christians. Teaching and preaching forgiveness are ineffective while harboring anger and resentment. Gwinn (2001) suggests that the teaching of forgiveness is best accomplished by modeling, not by lecture.

With these four good reasons for pastors to forgive, the notion that forgiveness is unimportant is clearly a myth, but simply debunking the popular myths about forgiveness is only a beginning. The effective pastor will need to substitute for the myths an accurate understanding of the forgiveness process in order to be better equipped to effectively practice a ministry of forgiveness.

THE FORGIVENESS PROCESS

Step 1: Decide

Forgiveness is a two-step process. Step one is the decision to forgive. This step is the responsibility of the human forgiver. Countryman (1998) writes, "So how do we go about forgiving? It begins when we make a choice to forgive" (p. 53). The decision to forgive is implemented by means of three focuses by the forgiver with regard to the injustice. Since forgiveness is first and foremost a decision, an understanding of the three is important.

Focus on the Truth

McCullough, Sandage, and Worthington (1997) advise those truly interested in forgiving not to gloss over or generalize the evil. The Old Testament hero of forgiveness, Joseph, was called upon to forgive his biological brothers who had sold him into slavery and given him up for dead. Later, when circumstances put Joseph in a position to punish the brothers, he chose instead to forgive them. He spoke clearly, focusing on the truth, when he said, "You intended to harm me . . ." (Genesis 50:20). Failing to focus on the truth may act to only suppress the pain and create even more devastating long-term effects.

Focus on the Cross

All forgiveness emanates from God's grace exemplified on the cross of Calvary. Appropriate a measure of that grace for the present decision. Some accomplish this by recalling Jesus saying about those who wronged him, "Father, forgive them . . ." (Luke 23:34). Some have even found it helpful to visualize Christ on the cross over the shoulder of the one who wronged them. They picture Jesus saying the words of forgiveness on their behalf until such time as they are able to speak forgiveness themselves.

Focus on the Future

Forgiveness leads to a brighter future. Forgivers focus on that future. They visualize the positive benefits of a restored relationship where that is possible and appropriate. When restoration is impossible, they focus on the liberation of leaving behind anger, bitterness, and malice.

Step 2: Be Healed

Once the decision to forgive is made and implemented, step two can begin in the pastor's life. This step involves a change in attitude and feelings. The forgiveness process is God's responsibility, and is totally accomplished by God's grace. "Forgiveness, by God or by people, is always from grace" (Gwinn, 2001, p. 90). The hurt and the pain of the injustice can only be soothed by the grace of God, but God refuses to begin that healing process until the decision to forgive is made and implemented.

Forgiveness difficulties arise when pastors and other forgivers expect a change in feelings, emotions, or attitudes to take place before the decision to forgive has been made. The two steps must be implemented in order. Pastor Karen said about a member of her congregation, "The hurt from his behavior is simply too deep. I can't forgive." She has the process reversed. In fact, the hurt is deep because the decision to forgive has not been made. Once that decision is behind her, Pastor Karen will discover God's grace begins the process of altering damaged emotions. Ketterman and Hazard (2000) relate from personal experience that forgiveness may be a long process that includes coming to understand other people and their feelings.

Of course, God's grace may not change the pain of injustices immediately. Some pastors report that they have to implement the decision to forgive again and again before the healing process is actually complete, which is another reason why they must begin forgiving as soon as possible following the injustice.

KEY CONCEPTS

The importance of forgiveness is often minimized by the prevalence of several myths about forgiveness. These include the following:

1. Forgiving is forgetting.
2. Forgiving is reconciling.
3. Forgiving is minimizing the offense.
4. Forgiving is taking the blame.
5. Forgiving is perpetuating injustice.
6. Forgiving is unimportant.

In response to the last myth, several reasons to forgive have been developed. These are:

- Forgiving improves spiritual well-being.
- Forgiving improves emotional well-being.
- Forgiving improves physical well-being.
- Forgiving improves pastoral effectiveness.

Pastors accomplish forgiveness by means of a two-step process. Step one is the human decision to forgive. Step two, the divine grace that heals the hurts of the past, is activated by step one. Individuals should forgive those who offend as soon as possible. The decision to forgive is implemented by:

- Focusing on the truth
- Focusing on the cross
- Focusing on the future

MEANINGS MANIA

Word Bank

a. forgiveness
b. reconciliation

Definitions

_____ 1. To give up resentment and anger for past injustices
_____ 2. To reunite or make one again

UNLEASHING THE POWER
OF INTERPERSONAL COMMUNICATION

Seamands (1981) suggests a three-test approach to determine if there is someone you need to forgive.

1. *Resentment test*

   List the people you resent. It may be a sibling, parent, extended family member, family friend, or co-worker. Many times these are people you have failed to forgive at some time in the past.

2. *Responsibility test*

   List the people you hold responsible for your current circumstances. The phrase "if only" often surfaces in the performance of this test according to Seamands. People you hold responsible for your current situation are in most cases people you should have forgiven at some point in the past.

3. *Reminder and reaction test*

   Who do you react negatively toward because he or she reminds you of someone else? List all those who fit in the "someone else" category. Chances are the people on that list have never been forgiven.

Take Seamands' tests honestly. Use the results to begin practicing the forgiveness process.

Chapter 12

Persuasion

Americans are exposed to more than 5,000 persuasive appeals every day (Larson, 2004). Candidates convince voters to cast a ballot for them in an upcoming election. Advertisers appeal to consumers that their product is superior to all others. Activists organize the citizenry to support their cause.

In addition to these universal persuasive appeals, pastors are bombarded with their own unique set of persuasive requests. Support your alma mater by sending a generous gift to the seminary. Encourage your congregation to get involved in the latest parachurch ministry. Stay abreast of the latest trends by attending the upcoming seminar. Enhance your interpretive skills by purchasing the hot-off-the-press book or subscribing to yet another clergy journal.

Thompson (1975) declares the primary reason to study persuasion lies in the fact that it is such an essential part of the real world. In addition, he suggests that the study of persuasion is valuable to those who are interested in:

- Advancing a cause
- Protecting themselves against unscrupulous persuaders
- Adjusting to and accommodating others

Certainly pastors are routinely engaged in each of these important activities. As a result, persuasion is an important part of a study of pastoral interpersonal communication.

THE NATURE OF PERSUASION

The study of persuasion is at least as old as the ancient Greek philosopher and scholar Aristotle. He defined rhetoric as the "ability in each cast to see the available means of persuasion" (Aristotle, 1991, p. 36). Others have expanded on the relationship between the spoken word and persuasion. For example, Burke (1969) believes that persuasion is "the use of symbols, by one symbol-using entity to induce action in another" (p. 46).

Fotheringham (1966), another highly respected communication scholar, shifted the emphasis from the source of the persuasive message to the receiver. He defines persuasion as "that body of effects in receivers, relevant and instrumental to source-desired goals, brought about by a process in which messages have been a major determinant of those effects" (p. 7). A synthesis of these and other definitions leads to an understanding of perception as the process whereby one individual attempts to elicit a voluntary change in the attitude or behavior of another. This definition reveals several key elements.

First, persuasion is a process. It utilizes the available means of communication to change another over time. In some situations a single word may be adequately persuasive, but in other situations the process requires a great deal of time and energy.

Second, persuasion involves a voluntary change. The process of persuasion is distinct from coercion. Holding a gun to someone's head in order to get him or her to accept the claims of Christ is neither persuasion nor effective evangelism.

Finally, persuasion involves a change in attitude and behavior.

- A pastor persuades a member of the community to change a long-held attitude about sleeping in on Sunday morning and adopt the behavior of attending church instead.
- A pastor persuades a member of the congregation to change his attitude about money and adopt the behavior of giving a tithe to the church.
- A pastor persuades a parishioner to change her attitude about time and adopt the new behavior of chairing the missions committee.
- A pastor persuades a colleague to change his attitude about competition and adopt a new behavior of support for ecumenical outreach.

In each of these situations it is clear that the process of persuasion may be chronologically protracted, in that the change in behavior may come some time after the change in attitude.

ETHICAL PERSUASION

Pastor Troy was deeply distressed when his denominational superior suggested he take a course in persuasion at the local community college as a part of his continuing education regimen. "I can't believe a Christian leader would recommend such a thing," Pastor Troy lamented. "What kind of a pastor would want to learn how to manipulate his flock?" Pastor Troy has mistaken persuasion with manipulation and has jumped to the false conclusion that all persuasion is unethical. Many who hold to a position similar to that of Pastor Troy have unwittingly confused persuasion with propaganda. Larson (2004) notes that the term propaganda originally meant to persuade people to accept the doctrine of the church. This came about when Pope Gregory XV began the "Sacred Congregation for Propagating the Faith" in 1622. Soon the word propaganda came to symbolize not only the tenets of the faith, but the communication strategies used to convince others of those beliefs. Sadly, the term propaganda today has negative connotations involving the use of strong emotional appeals and faulty reasoning. Perhaps Pastor Troy has mistaken persuasion for such a narrow and negative view of propaganda.

People can be ethical and persuasive at the same time. Johannesen (2002) suggests that there are several reasons to consider ethics and persuasion together. Among these is the notion that since persuasion involves impacting another's life, all the possible ethical ramifications should be considered. Whenever a communicator has an impact on the life of another, that communicator must be concerned about ethics.

Further, ethical considerations must be a part of any persuasive effort because persuasion involves choice. In order to be ethically persuaded, a person must be free to choose between alternative points of view. Violence or other coercive behaviors are not considered under the topic of ethical persuasion because they eliminate this important element of choice.

Although Pastor Troy is right to be concerned about ethics in the study of persuasion, he would do well to consider his superior's sound advice. Learning more about the elements and theories of persuasion does not automatically lead to unethical behavior. In fact, as Pastor Troy becomes more aware of persuasive techniques, he will be able to choose the most ethical approaches in his own advocacy, and will also be a more informed consumer of the persuasive appeal of others.

ELEMENTS OF PERSUASION

In Pastoral Conversation 12.1, Pastor Kyle is using what he knows about persuasion to recruit a chair for the church's committee on stewardship.

Pastoral Conversation 12.1

Background

The U. R. Welcome Sunday school class is holding their monthly class party at the local bowling alley. As usual, Pastor Kyle has joined the group. Pastor Kyle and Rhonda Bowland are sitting at the scorer's table waiting for their next turn on the lanes when the following dialogue takes place.

Dialogue

PASTOR KYLE: Rhonda, I've been meaning to talk to you about chairing the stewardship committee of the church next year.

RHONDA: Me?

PASTOR KYLE: Yes, you. As pastor, one of my responsibilities is to see that the very best people are nominated for each position. I think you have exactly the necessary skills to be stewardship chairperson.

RHONDA: Well, I don't know.

PASTOR KYLE: After all, you said recently that you are ready to get more involved in the church. Here's your opportunity.

RHONDA: I just never thought of myself as the chairperson type.

PASTOR KYLE: You're much too modest. Think it over. I'll call you next week.

Analysis

1. Has Pastor Kyle used an effective persuasive approach with Rhonda? Explain your answer.
2. What factors are likely to affect Rhonda's ultimate response?
3. Was it appropriate for Pastor Kyle to broach the subject in this setting? Defend your answer.

In reality, how Rhonda responds to Pastor Kyle's invitation to chair the committee can probably not be determined on the basis of this brief exchange. Her persuadability on the issue will depend in large part on several important variables. Andrews and Baird (2000) have identified four such variables as elements in the process of interpersonal persuasion.

Attraction is one variable that will determine whether or not Pastor Kyle has persuaded Rhonda to chair the committee. Attraction has to do with how Rhonda perceives Pastor Kyle in general. How similar does she perceive his views? Does she view Pastor Kyle as having the ability to provide personal rewards in this situation? Does she view him as an effective leader? Rhonda will subconsciously answer these and similar questions as she contemplates Pastor Kyle's request to "think it over."

A second variable in interpersonal persuasion, *status,* will also have a bearing on Rhonda's decision. People who are viewed as higher status and more expert on a subject are more likely to persuade. Rhonda's contemplation may also include questions about why Pastor Kyle sees her as having "exactly the necessary skills to be stewardship chair." She may subconsciously consider how well he has used evaluation skills in the past.

A third variable in interpersonal persuasion is *involvement.* Involvement refers to the depth and breadth of the relationship between the two participants in a potentially persuasive exchange. How well does Rhonda know Pastor Kyle? Does she trust him? What has been the nature of their previous pastor-parishioner interaction? The more positive Rhonda's answers to these questions, the more likely it is that she will be persuaded to serve as stewardship committee chairperson.

A final variable in interpersonal persuasion is *situation.* The physical environment of the bowling alley may make Pastor Kyle's appeal less persuasive. Similarly, the social context of a party may make it difficult for Rhonda to seriously consider her response, or ask appropriate follow-up questions. On the other hand, perhaps Pastor Kyle typically approaches the nominating task in a casual manner. If so, Rhonda may not even consider the environment as she formulates her response. Selection to a committee chair may be a prestigious honor in this particular church. If so, simply being asked may overshadow all other elements of the situation in Rhonda's thinking. If it is typical to take as committee chairpersons whoever will do the job, then Pastor Kyle's appeal is more likely to fall on deaf ears.

Students of persuasion generally agree that these four variables have a role in nearly every persuasive event. Agreement is not widespread, however, on exactly how the variables come together in order to allow a persuader to accomplish a particular persuasive agenda. As a result a variety of persuasion theories exist.

THEORIES OF PERSUASION

Ancient Theories

Aristotle was among the earliest and most influential of persuasive theorists. He believed that persuaders use proof to convince an audience of their point of view. He divided his study of proof into inartistic and artistic. Inartistic proofs are generally the result of a persuader's research. Statistics, examples, and quotations may be included in a persuasive appeal as an inartistic proof.

Aristotle was more interested in the artistic proofs or the art of persuasion itself. He identified three artistic proofs including ethos, pathos, and logos. *Ethos* refers to a persuader's credibility or character. Often whether a persuader has ethos will be a product of their past demonstrations rather than the message immediately at hand. Ethos is made up of wisdom, virtue, and goodwill. In Pastoral Conversation 12.1, Rhonda is more likely to accept Pastor Kyle's notion that she should serve as chairperson if Pastor Kyle has ethos. That is, if he has demonstrated wisdom, concern for all people, and genuine interest in Rhonda and other parishioners' well-being in the past.

Aristotle maintained that persuaders use not only ethos or credibility, but pathos as well. *Pathos* is the artistic proof that appeals to a person's emotions. Anger, fear, confidence, kindliness, pride, justice, and prudence are all used at one time or another by effective persuaders. Rhonda may take Pastor Kyle's conclusion that she is "obviously the right person for the job" as a source of great pride and a bolster to her self-esteem. In that case Pastor Kyle has used pathos effectively. If Rhonda sees the evaluation as empty flattery, Pastor Kyle has probably not been as effective in his use of pathos.

The third artistic proof of Aristotle is logos. *Logos* involves the use of the logical or rational argument. Much of Aristotle's work focused on the variety of rational appeals available to a persuader. When Pastor Kyle suggested to Rhonda that chairing the stewardship committee was her opportunity to get more involved, he used a logical appeal.

Although Aristotle was only one of several ancient theorists, his work is considered by many to be the most important and significant. He focused on public address as the most common setting for persuasion, but it is clear that his understanding has application in interpersonal settings as well.

These ancient theories suggest important ways to understand persuasion, but they are limited in their potential to explain (Borchers, 2002, p. 34). It fell to more modern theorists to more completely explain the process of interpersonal persuasion.

Needs Theories

Another group of theorists view persuasion in terms of the needs of the one to be persuaded. Thompson (1975) explains, "Motivation is a commonly held explanation of how changes are induced in attitudes, beliefs, and actions. Each individual has certain needs, motives, and habits, and he performs specific acts in accord with them" (p. 243).

Abraham Maslow is a key representative of the needs theorists. Maslow (1970) believed that people were persuaded according to their needs. He grouped human needs into five categories or levels, and maintained that lower level needs must be met before upper level needs afforded persuasive appeal.

The lowest level needs, which must certainly be met before an individual is susceptible to any higher appeal, Maslow termed physio-

lllll

logical needs. The need for air is a prime example. People who have the wind knocked out of them, and are thus is gasping for air are interested in nothing but their next breath. That need simply must be satisfied before any other needs serve to motivate or persuade.

Once physiological needs have been satisfied certain safety needs become prime motivators. The needs for food and shelter are representative of the safety needs.

The third level in Maslow's hierarchy of needs is termed belongingness or love needs. Every human being has the need to love and to be loved, but only when physiological and safety needs are satisfied does a person become motivated by love.

Esteem needs constitute the fourth level of the hierarchy of needs. Esteem needs are based on the innate desire of every human being to feel good about himself or herself.

Maslow's fifth and ultimate level of needs is identified as self-actualization needs. The person who has the need to be self-actualized has found satisfaction for needs in the lower four levels. His or her motivation is now focused on self-actualization or being the best that he or she can possibly be.

Pastor Irvin has a group of very enthusiastic college students in his congregation. Recently, one of them, Bart Tuttle, had a discouraging experience at the inner-city homeless shelter where he had gone to volunteer. An understanding of needs theory may help Pastor Irvin minister to Bart. The conversation is revealed in Pastoral Conversation 12.2

Pastoral Conversation 12.2

Background

Bart Tuttle stands in the doorway of Pastor Irvin's study after the midweek service. Usually upbeat and positive, Bart is clearly subdued.

Dialogue

PASTOR IRVIN: What's up? You look like you lost your best friend.
BART: No, but I didn't make any friends for the kingdom last night at Calvary Mission. I worked so hard on my devotion, and I really

thought it had lots of substance, but those guys at the shelter didn't think so. Half of them went to sleep and it was obvious the rest were just tolerating me because that's what they have to do to get a meal.

PASTOR IRVIN: I'm sure that it was discouraging, but sometimes ministry is like that. You will have more successes than you ever imagined over time.

BART: I sure hope so.

PASTOR IRVIN: Trust me, you will. By the way, what was the topic of your devotion?

BART: I titled it "Be All That You Can Be for Jesus." It was about the importance of reaching our full potential in the cause of Christ.

Analysis

1. What need level did Bart's devotion address? What need level would you expect to find at the homeless shelter? How could the differences explain Bart's lack of success?
2. What options does Pastor Irvin have for continuing the conversation with Bart? Which option would you suggest?

Consistency Theories

Another group of persuasion theories is called consistency theories. These theories are built upon the principle that human beings desire consistent thought patterns. Maintaining such consistency or escaping inconsistency becomes a strong motivating force.

Heider (1946, 1958) originally proposed the concept of cognitive consistency as a psychological goal within an individual. He viewed three elements as essential to the perception theory. Those included the perceiver, a second person, and an object. Heider (1946) believed that "the concept of balanced state designates a situation in which the perceived units and the experienced sentiments co-exist without stress" (p. 107). Heider's theory is very basic. It was left to those who built upon his work to apply balance theory to interpersonal relationships.

Newcomb (1961) was one of those who built upon Heider's model and applied it to the study of relationships. He based his understandings on interpersonal attraction as well as the need for consistency in relationships.

A situation at High Street Church serves to demonstrate the theories. Marge was delighted with the new pastor when she heard his first sermon, and when she participated in the midweek Bible study. "He is exactly what our church has needed," she enthusiastically said to a fellow member of the church. "Well, I don't know," came the hesitant response. "Did you know Pastor Kyle is divorced?" This new information forced Marge to a state of inconsistency since she strongly believed that clergy should never divorce. Marge must take action to retain consistency within herself. She has several possible courses.

- She could accept the reality of clergy divorce.
- She could force herself to believe that Pastor Kyle has not really been divorced.
- She could come to like Pastor Kyle less.
- She could learn to live with her internal inconsistency by declaring, "Clergy divorce is wrong; but Pastor Kyle is right for my church."

These earliest consistency theories tend to oversimplify reality since they reduce the communication act to two people and one topic or object. Most relationships are much more complex. The theories are instructive in that they suggest strategies for interpersonal persuasion based on the universal need of humans for cognitive balance.

Osgood and Tannenbaum (1955) propose another approach to the need for consistency in their congruency theory. Their understanding doesn't necessarily involve two persons, but two concepts or sets of information. If the two are congruent, there is balance. If they are dissimilar, there is pressure to change one or the other of the judgments.

Pastor Autumn was invited by her denominational leader to consider becoming the pastor at Kings Road Church. Kings Road was a rural congregation in the Midwest. It was also one of the fastest growing churches in the area. Pastor Autumn was not sure she wanted to apply because of her perception that rural churches have more trouble accepting women in ministry. She also believed that rural churches were usually stagnant or declining. The record clearly showed this church to be dynamic and growing. Such churches, Pastor Autumn believed, are more likely to respond to female leadership. Pastor Autumn was faced with finding some way to restore congruity in her attitude toward rural churches.

- She may change her attitude about rural churches.
- She may alter certain aspects of that attitude.
- She may dismiss the record of this particular church.

Festinger (1962) focused more on the power of imbalance in attitudes in his cognitive dissonance theory. According to his theory, dissonance is the feeling a person has when two beliefs do not match up. The striving to reduce such dissonance is a powerful persuasive force.

Pastor Mel was able to convince Dave Engels to become chairperson of the church's governing council by reminding him of his membership vow to be loyal to the church through service. Dave was very busy and did not see himself as a leader, but he also was an outspoken advocate of the importance of keeping one's word. He simply could not live with the dissonance of not keeping his own promise to serve. He thus eliminated the dissonance by making time, and by stretching his leadership skill. His opinion on integrity with regard to a vow was thus balanced with his own behavior.

Belief Hierarchy Theory

Although the consistency theories are helpful in developing a persuasive strategy, they share the problem that they tend to be too simplistic. Interpersonal persuasion cannot be reduced to the need for consistency in thinking alone. Other factors come together to help determine persuadability. One of these factors is explored in a theory by Rokeach (1973). His concepts are called belief hierarchy.

Rokeach noted that targets of persuasion do not hold all opinions with the same strength. Attitudes, beliefs, and values vary in strength and importance. A series of concentric circles helps model the concept (see Figure 12.1).

The core values within the inner circle are central to a person's being. Rokeach refers to these as primitive beliefs. They are developed by unanimous consensus. "The earth is round" is a primitive belief. So too is, "The sun sets in the west."

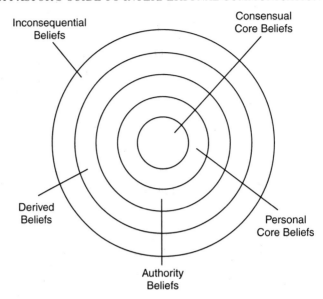

FIGURE 12.1. The Hierarchy of Beliefs

Level two beliefs are also labeled as primitive beliefs, but level two is distinguished from level one in that level two beliefs may have no general consensus. Level two beliefs are private and personal, but still as strongly held as level one. "Jesus is Lord," is an example of such a belief for many in the evangelical Christian community.

Level three or authority beliefs are learned over time by direct experience. They may be debatable and they may be changeable over time. Examples would be a pastor's belief that, "My greatest gift is preaching," or "I do the best ministry in a hospital setting."

Level four beliefs, which Rokeach labels derived beliefs, are developed from secondhand sources such as books, news broadcasts, or speakers as opposed to personal experience. A pastor's theological position is often a product of the seminary training that he or she experienced, for example. As a result, that position often fits into the category of derived belief.

Finally, level five encompasses inconsequential beliefs that are often called preferences or tastes. Whether a pastor makes hospital calls in the morning or the afternoon may be a product of this level of beliefs.

Rokeach maintains that a person may hold thousands of beliefs within each of the levels, which cluster to form attitudes. Attitudes in turn work together to develop values or courses of action. Although there may be shifts in attitudes, beliefs, and values in the short run as a result of the need for consistency, Rokeach argues that long-term persuasion comes only with a challenge to the entire value system of the individual.

Social Judgment-Involvement Theory

Sherif, Sherif, and Nebergall (1965) developed yet another theory that helps to explain the persuasion process. Their theory is known as social judgment-involvement theory. They refer to anchor points, which are those various internal reference points that a target of persuasion may hold. When a premise is posited, the target's latitude of acceptance includes the entire range of possibilities close to the anchor point, that is, those positions that the target already holds or could readily adopt.

Positions too far from the anchor point to even be considered are said to be in the latitude of rejection. The premise is so far outside the target's belief system that it cannot even be considered.

Between the latitude of acceptance and the latitude of rejection is the latitude of noncommitment. The range of noncommitment has the greatest possibility for persuasion to exist, since it is in this range that the target has not already decided either for or against a position.

In Pastoral Conversation 12.3, Pastor Jason is attempting to persuade a neighbor to attend his church. Apparently church attendance is well outside the neighbor's latitude of acceptance.

Pastoral Conversation 12.3

Background

Pastor Jason noticed that a house on Winter Street had new occupants. He stopped to welcome the new neighbors to the area. When Stacy Sauders came to the door the following conversation took place.

Dialogue

PASTOR JASON: Hi! My name is Jason Carson. I'm the pastor of the church on the corner. I noticed you were new to our neighborhood and wanted to stop and welcome you.

STACY: Well, thank you! That's very kind. My grandfather was a pastor.

PASTOR JASON: Really. Then you are familiar with the church. We would love to have you visit us Sunday morning at 9:30.

STACY: Oh yes, I suppose I am familiar with the church. That's why we probably won't be visiting, but I do appreciate your invitation.

Analysis

1. How should Pastor Jason respond to Stacy at this moment?
2. Based on this brief conversation is church attendance within Stacy's:

    Latitude of acceptance?

    Latitude of rejection?

    Latitude of noncommitment?

    What is the evidence for your answer? How would knowing which range church attendance falls in for Stacy affect Pastor Jason's follow-up activities?

Pastor Jason will need some time to get to know Stacy and her circumstances better. He may discover that:

- She comes from a very strict denominational group, and has rejected Pastor Jason's invitation because of his more liberal affiliations.
- An unduly strict grandfather has turned Stacy off toward anything or anyone associated with the church.
- A demanding and unappreciative congregation hurt Stacy's grandfather, whom she loved very much.

Each of these scenarios will require a different persuasive approach from Pastor Jason. Clearly, however, if he is to be successful in his persuasive attempt it will be because he takes the time and utilizes the energy necessary to get to know his new neighbor and her experience. Such are the demands of pastoral persuasive communication.

KEY CONCEPTS

Persuasion is a process designed to bring about a voluntary change in the attitude and behavior of another. As such it is an important aspect of a pastor's interpersonal communication. Persuasion is affected by interpersonal attraction, dominance, the breadth and depth of the relationship, and the situation surrounding the persuasive event.

Explanations of precisely how persuasion works are developed in a variety of persuasive theories. A sampling of these theories includes

- Ancient theories
- Need theories
- Consistency theories
- Belief hierarchy theory
- Social judgment-involvement theory

MEANINGS MANIA

Word Bank

  a. persuasion
  b. attraction
  c. status
  d. involvement
  e. social judgment-involvement theory
  f. situation
  g. ethos
  h. pathos
  i. logos
  j. hierarchy of needs
  k. cognitive consistency
  l. hierarchy of beliefs
  m. propaganda

Definitions

_____ 1. Persuasion variable whereby those with more expertise are more likely to persuade

_____ 2. The process that produces voluntary change in another's attitudes and beliefs

_____ 3. Abraham Maslow's theory that people are persuaded according to their needs

_____ 4. Usually thought of as very narrow, emotional, and manipulative

_____ 5. Rokeach theory that beliefs vary in strength and importance

_____ 6. Persuasion variable that considers likeability and effectiveness

_____ 7. Persuasion variable that considers breadth and depth of relationship

_____ 8. Credibility

_____ 9. Persuasion element that considers the circumstances surrounding the appeal

_____ 10. Sherif, Sherif, and Nebergall's theory built upon internal reference points

_____ 11. Consistent thought patterns

_____ 12. Rational appeal

_____ 13. Emotional appeal

UNLEASHING THE POWER
OF INTERPERSONAL COMMUNICATION

Copy or record a persuasive appeal from each of the following four sources.

1. A print ad from a magazine or newspaper
2. A television commercial
3. A radio commercial
4. An evangelistic sermon

Compare and contrast the persuasive approaches. In what ways are these persuasive mediums different from one another? How are they the same? Identify aspects of one or more of the theories described in this chapter in each of the four. In what ways is interpersonal persuasion different from these mass appeals? In what ways is it the same?

Chapter 13

Dual Relationships

Pastor Nelson had been at St. Thomas Church for just two weeks when Cliff Paterson, a laymember of the church, approached him with a concern. "Pastor, the lights were left on at the church on Sunday after everyone had gone," Cliff said.

Unsure of the significance of the revelation, Pastor Nelson fished a bit, "Has that been an ongoing problem at the church, Cliff?"

"I thought we had it pretty well under control with the former pastor, once it was made clear that it was his job to lock up and shut off the lights," Cliff responded.

"The pastor's job?" Pastor Nelson asked with genuine surprise.

"Of course," Cliff responded. "The pastor is here for every meeting and service anyway. It's a natural."

Obviously, Cliff and the folks at St. Thomas Church have confused the role of pastor with the role of custodian or building manager. As a result, Pastor Nelson will likely feel that he has been imposed upon, and taken advantage of. Cliff and those who share his thinking have violated an established boundary that presumably surrounds Pastor Nelson. The boundary has been established by the pastoral role. "Boundary violations between human beings occur when various roles are confused by either party or both parties" (Chirban, 1994, p. 50).

Of course, pastors are always expected to wear multiple hats. These legitimately include preacher, teacher, administrator, prophet, and comforter; yet, when a pastor's relationship with an individual person may be defined in terms of more than one role at the same time, problems can and do develop. In some cases the result may be no more serious than mild frustration such as that experienced by Pastor Nelson. At other times the blending of roles or blurring of role distinctions can lead to serious consequences.

The standard of ethical conduct for many professional groups such as those involved in counseling, psychotherapy, or social work forbid dual relationships. Dual relationships take a variety of forms, but always exist when a professional has another, usually personal relationship with a client. For example, many schools forbid faculty from developing a dating relationship with students. Similarly, counselors do not take family members as clients, and social workers do not go into business with persons on their caseload.

Focusing on the role of counselor, Montgomery and DeBell (1997) write, "Dual relationships are thought to be unethical because they cloud the clinical judgment of the counselor and may present conflicts of interest that prevent the counseling relationship from being beneficial" (p. 30).

Considering social work as the primary role, Kagle and Geibelhausen (1994) point out that

> a professional enters into a dual relationship whenever he or she assumes a second role with a client, becoming social worker and friend, employee, teacher, business associate, family member, or sex partner. . . . Dual relationships are potentially exploitative, crossing the boundaries of ethical practice . . . (p. 213)

The issue of dual relationships is of particular interest to pastors because much of the work of pastoral ministry potentially involves such relationships. For example, consider the dual relationship implications whenever a pastor becomes both pastor and

- therapist by entering a long-term counseling relationship with a parishioner.
- friend by hearing the confession of a friend from the congregation.
- a creditor or debtor by providing or receiving financial assistance from a member of the congregation.
- a supervisor by overseeing the work of a staff member or volunteer.
- a romantic partner by dating a parishioner.
- a former pastor by returning to a former parish to conduct a wedding.
- a wife by preaching with her spouse sitting in the congregation.
- a father by teaching his son's Sunday school class.

This chapter explores five dual relationships important to the typical pastor and offers suggestions for dealing with them.

PASTOR/COUNSELOR

Many people with emotional difficulties or personal problems seek counsel first from their rabbi, priest, or pastor (Weaver and Koenig, 1997). In fact, one study suggests that 39 percent of the public would use pastors for their counseling needs (Veroff, Kulka, and Douvan, 1981). Establishing a counseling relationship with a parishioner in many cases, however, constitutes the development of a dual relationship. This dual relationship can lead to professional dilemma and serious difficulties.

For example, Pastor Detrick conducted multiple-session counseling therapy for a member of his congregation who was experiencing difficulty with substance abuse. Later, that same parishioner was elected to the ministry committee of the church. In Pastor Detrick's church among other responsibilities the ministry committee has responsibility for evaluating the counseling ministry of the church. Both Pastor Detrick, as counselor, and the counselee found the situation uncomfortable and potentially embarrassing.

In another dual-role scenario, Pastor Sherri counseled with a single mother who was having problems with a rebellious teenage son. Later, Pastor Sherri preached on family and the Christian parent's responsibility. The former counselee believed that she had been singled out for ridicule as a result of the topic. She further suggested that Pastor Sherri had chosen illustrations that revealed confidences of their counseling sessions. In fact, Pastor Sherri had not even consciously considered the counselee's circumstances as she developed the sermon, but the previous dual relationship made it impossible to convince her accuser.

Pastor Millard perhaps faces the most serious challenge of all arising out of a pastor/counselor dual relationship. As a result of counseling with an adult female in his congregation, he learned that her own father had sexually abused her when she was a small child. The father was also a member of Pastor Millard's congregation and was a volunteer in the children's department of the Sunday school.

- If Pastor Millard does nothing, he risks violating the trust of the young children in his congregation.
- If Pastor Millard confronts the man about his past and asks him to resign, he betrays the confidence of the counselee.
- If Pastor Millard attempts to remove the man without explanation he undoubtedly will stir the ire of others in his volunteer-deficient Sunday school.

In each of these situations the dilemma could have been avoided had the pastor avoided multiple-session counseling situations. Krebs (1980) supports this view, arguing that pastors should not assume the role of professional counselor. Ochroch (1987) agrees and insists that one must choose between one of the two professional roles.

Disagreeing with this position, however, is the well-respected pastoral care expert Wayne Oates (1959). He maintains that the pastor does not have the choice of deciding whether or not to counsel, since people will inevitably bring their problems to their pastor. Switzer (1983) also takes a more lenient view by allowing the dual role of pastor/counselor to exist with certain limitations.

Limiting counseling to one or two sessions before professional referral minimizes both the differences between these experts, and the potential problems arising from the pastor/counselor dual relationship. Many pastors establish a very clear and well-publicized one or two session limit in advance of any emotional crisis. In addition, they develop and maintain a good working relationship with professional counselors who will readily accept their referrals.

Limited sessions does not allow for limited training, however. The pastor who intends to act as a counselor for even a few sessions has a moral and ethical responsibility to be well trained in the field of counseling or psychotherapy. Haug (1999) notes, "Many clergy have, in fact, expanded their traditional role of providing spiritual care and acquired *additional training* to function as counselors . . ." (p. 411, emphasis added).

In addition, even during these limited sessions, the pastor must take all necessary steps to maintain the pastoral role as primary. Parishioner/counselees should be made aware of potential dual-relationship problems and should be advised that their pastor intends to remain their pastor first and foremost.

PASTOR/LOVER

Members of the church are not willing to tolerate immoral or abuse-of-power relationships among members of the clergy. More arguable, however, are those instances of clergy sexual or romantic involvement with consenting parishioners of legal age. These represent the dual relationship of pastor/lover.

Generally, those involved in developing codes of ethics for counselors and psychotherapists have maintained the impropriety of the dual relationship of therapist and lover. "The codes of ethics of all major mental health professions explicitly prohibit sexual intimacies between counselor and client . . ." (Haug, 1999, p. 411). No such written code governs the practice of clergy, however, who are routinely engaged in helping, comforting, loving, and caring for parishioners. Such day-to-day activity can and does lead naturally to romantic involvements.

Pastor Steven was a single twenty-six-year-old appointed by the Episcopal leadership of his church to serve a small rural parish as his first postseminary assignment. Among the parishioners at this church was Joan, a recent college graduate, who was single and also in her midtwenties. Joan had returned to her hometown to take an elementary teaching position and became reinvolved in her home church. It didn't take long until some of the matchmakers in the congregation began to encourage Pastor Steven and Joan in a dating relationship. In fact, they needed little encouragement. In this particular case there were few complications to Pastor Steven's accepting the dual role of pastor and lover. After approximately a year of dating, the two were wed in an open-church ceremony officiated by a neighboring minister.

Not all pastor/lover dual relationships end so blissfully. Consider the following potential problems. What if:

- Either Pastor Steve or Joan had been previously married and in a denomination that forbids divorce and remarriage?
- Joan utilized her special relationship with Pastor Steve to gain social advantage among others at the church?
- Pastor Steve and Joan had been obviously involved in a physical relationship considered immoral by members of the congregation?

- The relationship between the two had not worked out, leaving either or both of them uncomfortable in the other's presence?
- Several other singles in the church had vied for Pastor Steve's attention?

Clearly the ideal course of action is for the pastor to avoid dual relationships. Single pastors may want to indicate prior to their employment their intention to not date within the congregation. Such an announcement not only helps fend off potential partners, and the inevitable in-church matchmakers, but also helps establish an accountability network for the pastor.

PASTOR/FAMILY MEMBER

The third dual relationship, that of pastor/family member, is more complex than the first two because many congregations expect their pastor's family to also be a part of the congregation. Laypeople, as a rule, have little understanding of, or appreciation for, the concept of dual relationships. For them, the idea of a "pastoral family" is not unlike the concept of the "first family" in American culture. Traditionally, Americans simply expect the president's spouse and children to occupy the White House and participate in State activities.

On the other hand, to be a pastor and a spouse, or pastor and a parent to the same person is at times difficult if not impossible. Pastoral Conversation 13.1 points to just one of the potential pitfalls.

Pastoral Conversation 13.1

Background

Pastor Robbie and his wife, Veronica, are the parents of a sixteen-year-old son, Toby. Over the past several months they have been having increasing difficulty communicating with Toby. Most of the time he is distant and quiet. When they have been able to engage him in conversation, Toby has been argumentative and belligerent. The following conversation took place between Pastor Robbie and Veronica after a confirmation class for the twelve-year-olds at the church.

Dialogue

VERONICA: How did the class go?

PASTOR ROBBIE: Pretty well, except for a troubling statement from one of the kids.

VERONICA: More sarcastic comments?

PASTOR ROBBIE: No, not at all. We were discussing the fact that Christians believe that their bodies are the Holy Spirit's dwelling place. As a result we avoid certain harmful practices.

VERONICA: That sounds like a good discussion to me.

PASTOR ROBBIE: It was. I just let the kids talk among themselves about some of the harmful practices they have witnessed among the older kids.

VERONICA: And . . .?

PASTOR ROBBIE: As they discussed alcohol and drug abusers, Toby's name came up along with several other boys from the church.

Analysis

1. How reliable is the information that Pastor Robbie has uncovered? What should he do with the information? How has a dual role led to this dilemma?
2. If Pastor Robbie confronts Toby, what impact will the confrontation have on Toby's view of the church? Can Pastor Robbie as a parent fail to confront Toby? Explain your answer.
3. What should Pastor Robbie do with the information about the other boys in the church? How does your answer differ when you consider his role as parent and his role as pastor?

Pastors and their families who decide to maintain the dual role of pastor/family member will want to take special care to safeguard both relationships. Considerations include

- The congregation should be educated and frequently reminded of the special relationship.
- Families should always have available, in the form of clergy from a neighboring parish or denominational official, those who will act as a substitute in providing pastoral care.

- Pastors should carefully consider in advance which relationship takes priority in the event of a dual-relationship crisis.
- Pastoral support and accountability groups should be in place to help hold pastors accountable in the midst of the dual relationship.
- In situations in which the church and the pastoral family can agree, the dual relationship should be escaped as soon as possible.

PASTOR/FRIEND

Someone once quipped that a friend is "someone who knows you very well and likes you anyway." Since that definition could also describe the role of a pastor, one might argue that no dual role exists but instead the role of friend is really an enhancement of the role of pastor. A friend, however, is someone who is united to another to form an alliance. A friend is an ally. Certainly pastors, as with all human beings, need good allies. An alliance with a parishioner, however, is a dual relationship that can lead to some boundary dilemma.

Pastor Greg developed a close personal friendship with Ken, a member of his own congregation. The two played golf together several times a week. In addition, along with their spouses, they had begun to meet frequently for dinner or some other social engagement. Pastor Greg was aware that many pastors and clergy ethicists advised against friendships within one's own congregation. As a measure of precaution he had therefore set a boundary early in the friendship. "We never talk about the church," he had insisted of Ken. The limitation didn't seem to harm the friendship because the pair had much more in common. Ironically it was that very limitation that led to difficulties for Ken in the relationship. Members of the congregation saw Ken as a channel by which to communicate with Pastor Greg. "He just needs to know that the topic he selected is not very exciting for the adult retreat," one man told Ken. Another parishioner encouraged, "I wish you would let Pastor Greg know when you see him that Mrs. Jones is in the hospital." Another messenger declared, "There's a new family on Vine Street that Pastor Greg should call on. Be sure to tell him when you see him." On and on went the message sending that Ken was forced to listen to and ignore. Ultimately, the uncomfortable position affected not only the friendship, but communication within the parish.

Another situation in which a pastor participated in the dual role of friend produced a much different but equally negative result. Pastor Colleen became close personal friends with Amanda, a member of her congregation. The extent of the negative impact became clear one evening as the employment committee of the church met to evaluate the work of Pastor Colleen. Pastoral Conversation 13.2 reveals the circumstances.

Pastoral Conversation 13.2

Background

The employment committee has just completed its semiannual written review of Pastor Colleen. As required by church governance, committee members are reviewing the evaluation document with Pastor Colleen before sending it on to the denominational headquarters.

Dialogue

PASTOR COLLEEN: I see that you have agreed on a fairly low mark in pastoral visitation. Could someone help me understand that better?

MARY ANNE: Well, it's just that we think there are shut-ins and occasional attendees who would benefit from more attention from the pastor.

SAM: We need to be totally honest, Mary Anne. It's more than that.

ESTHER: I agree. We think our pastor spends entirely too much time visiting with one or two people, while ignoring the rest of the flock.

PASTOR COLLEEN: Now I'm really confused. Ignoring? Too much time with a few?

SAM: It looks to us like you do plenty of visitation at Amanda's house, but the rest of the church goes wanting.

PASTOR COLLEEN: But Amanda and I are friends.

ESTHER: Well, I never . . . What in the world are the rest of us?

MARY ANNE: What Esther means, Pastor, is that we hope everyone in the church is your friend.

Analysis

1. Should Pastor Colleen reveal this conversation to Amanda? What are the implications for friendship if she does or does not? What are the implications with regard to pastoral ethics either way?
2. How should Pastor Colleen respond to the committee?

Clearly the dual role of pastor/friend raises some boundary issues that cannot be ignored. Some have maintained that loneliness among the clergy is such a critical problem that the risk may be ethically taken (Honstead, 2004). If dual relationships are unethical, they remain so even in the midst of loneliness. Support roles are necessary, but should be maintained and developed outside the congregation.

Not everyone agrees with this limitation, however. For example, Wells (2004) writes, "Not only is it okay for pastors to have friendships within their parishioners and with other clergy, it is absolutely essential" (p. 16). Wells attempts to sidestep the problems of the dual role by creating a new term, "holy friendship."

> Holy friendships may not look different to the outside world. But what sets them apart is that they have a larger purpose beyond the friendship itself: they help point us toward God. Holy friendships are about truth telling, encouragement, and accountability. (p. 17)

Surely friendships between Christians should always be of the nature described by Wells, yet creating a term does not eliminate the problems of the dual relationship. Whether the dual relationship is pastor/friend, or pastor/holy friend, the problems persist.

It seems most advisable for the pastor to plan to maintain personal friendships only outside the congregation. Simple logistics can mean a problem for pastors. More time is actually spent with parishioners in the performance of pastoral duties. As a result, other relationships will need to be very intentional. Yet the dual-relationship problems are critical enough to make the extra effort worthwhile.

PASTOR/FORMER PASTOR

Although the first four dual relationships involve a pastor's relationship with parishioners, the dual relationship of pastor/former pastor has more to do with former parishioners and their new pastor. Ethical and effective pastors avoid the dual role of being a pastor and a former pastor to a congregation.

Pastor Juan was a very popular leader of Grace Church for six years. When his Episcopal leader moved Pastor Juan to a new setting in another part of the region, Juan greeted the change with mixed emotions. The members at Grace Church, however, were nearly unanimous in their opinion that Pastor Juan should remain. They believed that no one could ever adequately replace him. Not surprisingly then, the members of Grace Church sought to stay in contact with Pastor Juan. At first the cards and letters offered only personal information about family or the community. As time passed, however, Pastor Juan began to hear more and more criticism of his successor. Clearly members of Grace Church were airing their frustrations about their church leader with Pastor Juan. The matter came to a head when Pastor Juan was asked to perform the funeral for an aged member of Grace Church who had died.

Most pastoral care professionals agree that Pastor Juan should decline to be involved in the ministry of his former church. Pastor Juan's current assignment should occupy enough of his professional time without his attempting to also be the pastor of a former church. In addition, Pastor Juan owes to his successor the professional courtesies of support and encouragement.

Undoubtedly, the members of Grace Church will persist. "How can you just quit caring about us?" they might ask. "Don't we have the right to choose who will bury our parents or marry our daughters?" "This is a special case; since you buried Dad when you were our pastor, we want you to bury Mom, too."

The ethical pastor will remain firm regardless of the pressure. It is inappropriate and ineffective to be a pastor and a former pastor at the same time. A few simple guidelines assist in maintaining the boundary.

1. Let the congregation know what to expect prior to a move. Part of the termination statement described in Chapter 8 should be a

clear communication advising that a former pastor returning to play the pastoral role is inappropriate and should not be anticipated.

2. Support successors wholeheartedly. Never engage in negative conversation about a successor. Refuse to listen to criticism about him or her from others.

3. Visit a former parish only upon the invitation of the current pastor. In some locales former pastors return for homecoming and similar situations. At these events the role of "former pastor" is a revered and thus enjoyable position. Many current pastors want to allow colleagues in ministry that privilege. In every case, however, the propriety of a return visit should be left to the judgment of the current pastor.

4. Don't waver. Parishioners can find a multitude of reasons to encourage former pastors to violate the ethical boundaries.

> We don't attend that church anymore.
> You're retired, not moved to another congregation.
> We haven't found a pastor yet.
> You've always been special to our family.
> The wedding is at the house, not at the church.
> The funeral is at the funeral home, not at the church.
> The current pastor told us it was okay to ask.

In spite of the rhetoric, an inappropriate dual relationship exists when a former pastor attempts to be a pastor. Thus ethical pastors will carefully avoid the dual relationship. Yet they may still have to deal with the unethical dual relationship of their own predecessors, which is the dilemma in Pastoral Conversation 13.3.

Pastoral Conversation 13.3

Background

Pastor Wade served the Westminster Church for six years. When the Episcopal leader of the area instructed him to prepare to move to another church, Pastor Wade withdrew his membership in the denomination, rented a storefront in the community, and started his own independent church. Pastor Al was subsequently assigned to Westminster. Pastor Al has had a good beginning in the three months since he came to Westminster, although attendance is down about 30 percent because of those who are attending the new independent church led by Pastor Wade. The following exchange took place in a hospital corridor where Pastor Al has come to visit a parishioner.

Dialogue

PASTOR AL: Hello, Wade. How are you?

PASTOR WADE: Fine, Al. How are things at Westminster?

PASTOR AL: We're doing well, thank you.

PASTOR WADE: I bet you're here to see Roberta Simmons. I've just come from her room. She's doing much better, but I'm sure she will be glad to see you.

PASTOR AL: I would expect so. I am her pastor. But why are you calling on her?

PASTOR WADE: I try to keep in touch with old friends, of course. And then again, if people want to become a part of a new and exciting ministry, I'm not likely to stand at the door with a gun to drive them away.

Analysis

1. How should Pastor Al respond to Pastor Wade?
2. Should Pastor Al go ahead with his planned visit to Roberta Simmons? If so, should he ask Roberta about Pastor Wade's visit?
3. What is the best overall approach to counteract the unethical behavior of Pastor Wade? What approaches are not likely to be effective? Why?

The behavior of former Pastor Wade is clearly unethical. Yet most experienced pastors would suggest that Pastor Al should avoid trying to teach ethics to his predecessor. If Pastor Al responds with outrage, that action will only serve to further endear Pastor Wade to those parishioners who are already inclined to follow him. In fact, one pastor who found himself precisely in Pastor Al's situation recommended "killing him with kindness." He reasoned, "If my own strengths have not made me the pastor in six months, it's probably not going to happen anyway." Sadly, too many pastors lack the necessary self-confidence to respond in such a way.

PREVENTIONS

Most pastoral ethicists agree that avoiding dual relationships is the most ethical approach to boundary dilemma. Gula (1996) summarizes that "dual relationships can be inappropriate and even wrong because they are fertile ground for impairing judgment, harboring potential conflicts of interest, and exploiting the trust and dependency of the vulnerable" (Gula, 1996, p. 83).

The effective pastor will want to minimize the dual-relationship problem that so easily undermines ministry. Dual relationships can most easily be avoided by a series of preventive actions. The following five action steps help the pastor avoid the pitfalls of dual relationships.

Action Step 1: Code of Ethics

Good ethical decisions are usually not made on the spur of the moment. Wise pastors develop a code of ethics including appropriate boundaries in advance. Write out the code of ethics, take it under advisement with other pastors, and revisit the statement often.

Action Step 2: Accountability

"Building supportive professional networks to reduce professional isolation and increase accountability serves to reduce the threat of dual relationships" (Haug, 1999, p. 420). An accountability group can serve to question relationships and help a pastor get out of dual relationships before they become a problem. An accountability group may also serve a monitoring function when dual relationships are impossible to avoid.

Action Step 3: Self-Care

Maintaining fulfilling appropriate relationships professionally and personally minimizes the possibility that a pastor will be blindsided by the development of a dual relationship. For example, a pastor should have a working relationship with a professional counselor. This allows the pastor to make acceptable referrals routinely. In addition, the pastor should nurture quality friendships outside the congregation in order to avoid a potentially damaging pastor/friend dual relationship.

Action Step 4: Self-Awareness

Pastors should be aware of their own needs and urges. Although parishioners may view pastors as safe, superhuman, and knowledgeable about setting limits, the wise pastor recognizes his or her own limitations in boundary selection and enforcement (Hart, 1982). Such awareness naturally leads to focused prayer and the recruitment of key allies when a dual relationship threatens.

Action Step 5: Education

Congregations must be educated in the potentially destructive nature of pastoral dual relationships. The educational process must be in advance of the development of a dual relationship. As a result, parishioners often become allies in the avoidance of such relationships. For example, recognizing the ethical issues involved in dual relationship may cause a parishioner to seek counsel elsewhere, or to resist the temptation to call a former pastor for pastoral services such as the performance of weddings or funerals.

KEY CONCEPTS

Most helping professions have a strongly worded code of ethics that discourages the development of dual relationships. Pastors should also pay careful attention to the avoidance of some significant dual relationships. These include the role of pastor blended with the role of:

- Counselor
- Lover
- Family member
- Friend
- Former pastor

The wise pastor implements a series of preventive actions steps before dual relationships even become an issue. Such preventive measures include

- Code of ethics
- Accountability
- Self-care
- Self-awareness
- Education

MEANINGS MANIA

Word Bank

a. dual relationship
b. code of ethics
c. boundaries
d. accountability

_____   1. The limits to a relationship established by the role of the participants
_____   2. A written statement of propriety
_____   3. Relationship where a professional has a personal relationship with a client or parishioner
_____   4. Professional networks designed to reduce isolation and the threat of impropriety

UNLEASHING THE POWER OF INTERPERSONAL COMMUNICATION

Write a preliminary code of ethics for pastoral ministry. Be sure your statement encompasses at least the five dual relationships discussed in this chapter. Review your statement with an experienced pastor. What aspects of pastoral ethics does she or he see as significant? Revise your statement as necessary.

Chapter 14

Pastor, Partner, Parent

Franklin Graham, son of the best-known clergyman of the twentieth century, recalls his parents' attitude toward raising children under the glare of the limelight.

> They knew much more clearly than I did the pressures I faced being a "preacher's kid" as well as the oldest son of a "Christian legend." I'm sure God gave them wisdom to know that if they pushed me too hard to conform, I might take off running and never come back—not just away from them, but perhaps from God too. (Graham, 1995, p. 53)

Not all pastoral families experience such wisdom. Nor do all realize such positive results. Anderson (1998) discovered that of 487 respondents who grew up as the children of clergy, nearly half reported a time when they rebelled against the church, and 68 percent admitted to having felt rebellious against the church.

One preacher's kid (PK) reported being turned off to the church for many years after her adolescence. Her preacher father, in an attempt to guarantee conformity and insulate himself from the criticism of the church, forced her to read the Bible for punishment. "I vowed," she recalls, "when I get out of this situation I'm never coming back. I'll never read that book again."

Fortunately, not all communication in pastoral families turns out so tragically, but in nearly every case some difficult communication obstacles must be overcome. A clear relationship exists between these pastoral family communication issues and pastoral communication in the church. Lee and Balswick (1989) believe that "The quality of a pastor's ministry cannot be neatly separated from his or her interpersonal or family life" (p. 7). Similarly, Wynn (1960) points out that interpersonal difficulties in a pastor's family can affect the entire church. And the

Apostle Paul advises the young pastor Timothy with a rhetorical question, "If anyone does not know how to manage his own family, how can he care for God's church?" (1 Timothy 3:5).

Lee and Balswick (1989) point out that pastoral families are not necessarily unique. The social environment in which they function is what is unique. The pastor who seeks to improve communication within his or her own family would, therefore, benefit from a study of one or more of the plethora of general works available on the subject. For example Burns (2003), Harley (2001), Rainey (2002), Rekers (1985), Stafford (2004), Stanton (2004), and Smoke (2004) all have beneficial information for every family including pastoral families. This chapter is limited to a study of issues arising from that unique social environment in which the pastoral family exists. The environment is examined through pitfalls in pastoral family communication, and through the unique resources available to pastoral families to assist them in overcoming these pitfalls.

PITFALLS TO PASTORAL FAMILY COMMUNICATION

Recognizing the five common pitfalls to quality pastoral family communication will assist the pastoral family in overcoming their potentially deadly impact.

Fatigue and Time Pressure

Pastor David Seamands and his wife, Helen, were asked for their number-one rule for raising a family in a ministry setting. They responded, "The number one rule is to make your marriage and your family a top priority. This means planning prime time together as a couple and as a family" (Seamands and Seamands, 1981, p. 23). The Seamands' response indicates the extent of pastoral family stress arising from fatigue and time pressure.

Just the usual pace of life ensures that most twenty-first-century American homes suffer from fatigue and time pressure. However, the twenty-four-hour call and the intense demands of pastoral responsibility accentuate such stress in the parsonage home. Although most professionals practice only at the office or clinic, and within certain prearranged time blocks, pastors are expected to be available whenever they are needed. In addition, the time demands in pastoral ministry are not consistent from one day to another, but vary with such issues as the number of parishioners in the hospital or the season of the Christian year. This makes it extremely difficult to maintain consistent blocks of family time. Although many parishioners are sensitive to pastors' personal and family time needs, some are not, as Pastor Abby discovered in Pastoral Conversation 14.1.

Pastoral Conversation 14.1

Background

Walking into the church office on a Thursday morning, Pastor Abby feels renewed and refreshed as a result of yesterday's rest. After several weeks of coordinating schedules, she was able to get a key layperson to lead the midweek service, and her husband, Mike, took a vacation day from his work. She and Mike had gone with their two children for a quiet fun-filled day at the beach. Karen, the church secretary, greets Pastor Abby as she arrives.

Dialogue

KAREN: Good morning, Pastor. How was your day off?

PASTOR ABBY: It was wonderful. Mike and I agreed on the way home that we have to take more days like that. Do you know that is the first day off we've had together in six weeks?

KAREN: I do know, Pastor. But I'm afraid everyone doesn't.

PASTOR ABBY: What do you mean?

KAREN: Lynda Palmer called yesterday to ask you to give the invocation for the PTO [Parent-Teacher Organization] carnival at seven o'clock last evening. I told her I doubted if you would have been able to arrange that even if you'd been in town yesterday since the midweek service begins at seven.

PASTOR ABBY: Sounds right to me.

KAREN: Not to Lynda. In her words, "It's bad enough that the pastor is lollygagging around in the middle of the workweek, but she doesn't even care enough about public relations to make the PTO carnival a priority." She wants you to call her first thing.

Analysis

1. How should Pastor Abby respond to Lynda?
2. What can Pastor Abby do to minimize the negative reactions she got to a day off?
3. Should Pastor Abby mention the reaction of Lynda to her husband? What impact will Lynda have on Pastor Abby's family if she does? What impact will she have if Pastor Abby keeps the matter to herself?

The potential for damage to pastoral children who suffer from the starvation of parental time is enormous. Nicholi (1985) notes the increase of suicide, violent crime, drug use, eating disorders, and depression among adolescents from the 1950s through the 1980s. He maintains that changes in the amount of time that parents spend with their children directly correlates with the rise in these and other antisocial behaviors. If Nicholi is correct, pastors must find ways to overcome fatigue and time pressure and spend more time developing positive lines of communication in the parsonage home.

Pastors and their spouses will need to be particularly attentive to guard against three myths that many use to rationalize their lack of family time priority (Neff, 1995). The first myth is, "I don't have time." In reality everyone has the same amount of time. The problem is priorities, not amount of time.

The second myth is that quality time makes up for quantity time. In fact, families need both quality and quantity time from all parents, including pastoral parents.

The third myth is the myth of materialism. Providing *things* does not compensate for providing *time*. This myth becomes especially prevalent in dual-career homes in which pastors add a full-time job to their pastoral workload.

Pastors and their families can offset the negative effects of fatigue and time pressure by practicing a family night at home (Ratcliff, 1995). Many pastors have discovered that when a day off or a family night are publicized within the congregation, members respect and honor the pastoral family's need for time alone. In some churches the concept has spread to the families of laity. In these churches, no church meetings or events are scheduled on one consistent and prearranged night each week. All families are thus encouraged to spend time at home in family interaction.

Another way for pastoral families to overcome the time demands of ministry is to celebrate individual family members. In many pastoral homes a regular date night, not only with spouse but with individual children, has lessened the impact of fatigue and time pressure on family communication.

Pastoral families should develop common interests. The negative impact of fatigue and time pressure is intensified when family members have no common interests with which to enjoy free time together. Making the interests of a child one's own maximizes the benefits of that free time that is available, and emphasizes the child's self-worth at the same time. Couples must be careful to develop common interests beyond the raising of children. This helps avoid a later crisis precipitated by the empty nest.

Pastors who are intent on overcoming the negative impact of pastoral time demands will always maintain family vacations. Every pastor is entitled to time away from the demands of the parish. Pastors benefit the most who recognize such time as an act of love toward the parsonage family. Often pastors discover benefits from planning the vacation sufficient distance away so that "emergency" returns are impractical.

In addition, those pastoral families most successful at overcoming fatigue and time pressure are those who share the work. Many successful pastoral families have attacked the time demands that lead to fatigue and time pressure by developing a sense of team ministry. Even the youngest children can fold bulletins, staple newsletters, or pray simply for those who are sick. "The happiest and the most useful parsonage families are where there is total involvement in the work of the church. Everyone, yes, including the children see themselves as part of the team" (Taylor, 1989, p. 53).

Whatever procedures the pastor and pastoral family develop in order to maintain family time, the number one rule at the Seamands' house is vitally important for all pastoral families. The pastor must give the family a place of priority second only to his or her relationship to God. After all, "If anyone does not provide for his relatives, and especially for his immediate family, he has denied the faith and is worse than an unbeliever" (1 Timothy 5:8).

Financial Pressure

A second pitfall that interrupts communication lines in pastoral families stems from low salaries. In a study by Lee and Balswick (1989) ministers' spouses listed inadequate financial income as the most severe problem associated with the pastoral profession. In the same study, for the pastors themselves, only inadequate time for family constituted a greater issue than the pressures of finance. Clearly, financial pressures constitute a major source of pastoral family stress.

The rising cost of higher education intensifies this pressure, especially on younger clergy families. In one recent year the average cost of tuition and fees at a four-year public school exceeded $4,000, while room and board added $5,500 more (Cannon, 2003). Since theological seminaries are not publicly funded in the United States, the costs are usually significantly higher, and rising more sharply. As a result, the typical first-year pastor who has a four-year undergraduate degree and a Master of Divinity degree may have already invested $125,000 or more in education. In many pastoral families that means a staggering load of debt to be maintained on what has traditionally been among the lowest of professional salaries.

This scenario has led to a change in attitudes about debt among pastoral families. For example, since the days of John Wesley those seeking ordination in the United Methodist Church have been asked by the presiding bishop to respond to a series of questions before the annual conference. No wonder that in recent years the traditional question, "Are you in debt so as to embarrass you in your work?" has been greeted with nervous chuckles.

One reminder that laypeople sometimes offer as compensation for low pastoral salaries is the addition of a parsonage to the package. Not having to pay rent or make a house payment, especially in the earliest years of a pastor's ministerial career, constitutes a tremendous cash-flow benefit, and a utilities package is always advantageous. Yet many pastors in their middle and later years are discovering that free housing that ends at retirement is a mixed blessing. A home is the single greatest investment for the average family, making the requirements of cash flow in retirement only 75 to 80 percent of the amount needed during the mortgage repayment years. By contrast, the parsonage system guarantees that a retiring pastor will need

125 percent or more of the last working salary in order to provide housing and maintain an unchanging standard of living.

In short, from beginning to end, a pastor's career is likely to be fraught with financial pressures. These pressures can have enormous negative impact in the communication patterns of a pastoral family.

Faulty Expectations

Everyone relates to others on the basis of image. The congregation has an image of "pastor." They relate to the person bearing that title on the basis of that image. No problem exists when that image matches the pastor's self-image and when the pastor is able to adequately accomplish the mutually agreed role. A pitfall develops when a pastor is unable to exact the role. "The dangerous practices of . . . conforming to roles which are not real all have a devastating effect on marriage" (Lavender, 1986, p. 113). Yet pastors inevitably are faced with unrealistic expectations in the course of their work.

Many pastors are willing to accept faulty expectations as just an occupational hazard. They understand and adjust to the fact that everyone does not have the same understanding of the role of pastor. A more serious issue develops when the entire pastoral family is placed upon an unachievable pedestal through faulty expectations. In Pastoral Conversation 14.2, an expectation of the role of Pastor Mick's wife could have serious consequences for the church as well as Pastor Mick's family.

Pastoral Conversation 14.2

Background

Pastor Mick has been the Pastor of Trinity Church for six months. Although Pastor Mick enjoys the small-town setting and his work at Trinity, his wife, Sherry, has not been as comfortable. Having grown up in the city, she has found the small town and small church stifling. She and Mick are excited about her recent job as church organist in a large metropolitan church only an hour's drive away. On this, the first Sunday that she is away to fulfill the responsibility of her new position, Mick is visiting after the Trinity service with parishioner Josh Sigmond, a key Trinity layman.

Dialogue

JOSH: Great service this morning, Pastor.

PASTOR MICK: Thanks, Josh.

JOSH: Tell Sherry we missed her. Is she sick this morning?

PASTOR MICK: No, she's fine. In fact, she's very excited. She got a great opportunity to play for a large church in the city. I'm anxious to see how it went for her.

JOSH: You mean she's filling in for a Sunday?

PASTOR MICK: Well, we hope not. She'd like to have the job permanently.

JOSH: You need to think that one through carefully, Pastor. I'm not sure how Trinity Church will react to never seeing the pastor's wife on Sunday morning.

PASTOR MICK: I thought we had mutually agreed that the church was hiring me, and there would be none of this "two for the price of one" stuff.

JOSH: That's true. It's not like we expect her to play the organ here for free. We already have great musicians. But what kind of a pastor's wife doesn't even attend the church?

Analysis

1. How should Pastor Mick answer Josh's question?
2. Is Sherry's job appropriate in your opinion? Give reasons to support your response.
3. Are there ways Pastor Mick might have prepared the congregation for the change? Would such preparation make a difference in the congregation's response?

Douglas (1961) refers to the problem evidenced at Trinity Church as the "royal family complex." He notes that in a monarchy the royal family is given love and respect without earning it, strictly on the basis of who they are. The price is that the royal family is expected to be the exemplars of the culture. In the pastoral royal family the expectation is that the pastoral family will be exemplars of morality, child rearing, couple communication, civic leadership, and every aspect of spiritual development. Apparently at Trinity Church, and in many other traditional churches in America, the royal family is expected to attend worship together.

The royal family complex is particularly demanding on PKs, who live with the combination of double standard and negative expectations (Bouma, 1981). PKs are expected to be better than other kids. Such double-standard expectations come from both adults and peers within the congregation and community, and sometimes even from the pastoral parents themselves, who see any youthful indiscretion on the part of the youngster as an indictment on their own pastoral and parental success. Many parishioners seem to have particularly low expectations with regard to the behavior of PKs. The offspring of pastors are assumed to be unruly, hard to handle, and rebellious.

Lee (1992) observes, "There is a terrible irony in this. On the one hand, the pastor's children are expected to display exemplary Christian behavior. . . . On the other hand even when they fulfill these expectations, their motivations and initiative are questioned" (p. 25). Whether the expectations are of pastor, pastor's spouse, or PK the pressure to meet faulty expectations can have devastating effects on the pastoral family.

Frequent Moves

Most families, when experiencing periodic stress, find allies in the deep extrafamily relationships that they have developed over time. Pastoral families may discover they have little support, however, because frequent moves have left them with very shallow roots and only superficial friendships. McBurney (1985), in analyzing the stress on one pastoral family, notes, "The pastor and spouse felt like transients, migrant workers. This created stress, and it occurred because the migrants didn't take the time—or get the time—to settle in and belong" (p. 80).

Traditionally, pastors have transferred from one location to another more frequently than professionals in other areas. Each year 25 percent of all pastors, or an average of more than 100 pastors a day, experience a move (Lavender, 1986). That number is increased by the presence of the highly centralized denominations in the data. These groups tend to move pastors more frequently. Yet, even among more decentralized and independent churches, transfers from one congregation to another are very common.

The impact of this transience is felt by adults in the typical stress of moving, and in the lack of deep friendships, but there may be even greater effects on pastoral children. Many parsonage children report that they feel geographically rootless. Even in young adulthood some PKs report having no "home" to return to. One PK reported that during his college years he made less frequent trips home than many of his classmates. A move during his senior year in high school had left him with no real friends from his high school graduating class with whom to socialize. In addition, the infrequency of his return "home" had a negative effect on his relationship with his pastoral parents during his young adulthood.

Many PKs emerge unscathed, however, and some even see benefits in the frequent moves. One adult who grew up in a parsonage home commented on her frequent moves. "I know people literally around the world as a result of my father's calling. I feel sorry for some of my friends who have never even met a single person who grew up outside their home state."

Fishbowl Existence

A final pitfall to pastoral communication grows out of the on-display aspects of the work. Pastoral ministry is a public profession. This is especially true in rural and small-town churches. One layperson explained her insistence that the pastor attend the community carnival by declaring, "We're proud of our pastor and just want an opportunity to show him off."

In another community a church matriarch insisted that the pastor attend her extended family's reunion with her and her husband. "I want the whole family to see what a fine preacher we have," she beamed.

In yet another situation, the pastoral family was less than amused when a nosey neighbor, who was also a church member, kept careful watch on who came and went from the parsonage. She gave frequent visitation updates to those in the congregation who would listen.

Without question this fishbowl existence is intensified when the pastoral family lives in a church-owned parsonage. Many church members reason that the parsonage belongs to them. As a result, it often becomes a convenient spot for overflow Sunday school classes, or babysitting for the morning service.

David and Helen Seamands (1981) recall coming home from a family vacation to discover that a tree in the yard of their parsonage home had been cut down. Closer investigation revealed that the hatchet man was a parishioner who was a neighbor. When they asked him about it, he explained that he did it because he simply didn't like the tree. Helen summarized, "Why not? The parsonage belongs to the congregation—that's the reasoning" (Seamands and Seamands, 1981, p. 18). The potential negative impact of this fishbowl existence on pastoral family communication is evidenced in Pastoral Conversation 14.3.

Pastoral Conversation 14.3

Background

Pastor Dan and his wife, Terri, are celebrating their first wedding anniversary. They have saved for several weeks to buy steaks for the occasion. They are just sitting down to a candlelit table when the doorbell rings. Pastor Dan opens the door to Gary Wright, the chair of the church trustees.

Dialogue

PASTOR DAN: Yes?

GARY: Good evening, Pastor. Hope I'm not disturbing . . .

PASTOR DAN: Well, we were—

GARY: (interrupting) I need to walk through the parsonage. As chairman of the trustees I have to report on the parsonage condition to the denominational officials.

PASTOR DAN: Of course. When would you like to schedule that?

GARY: I thought I would just take a quick look around right now. I've got lots going on. When I do get a free moment I like to use it wisely.

PASTOR DAN: Well, we were just sitting down to dinner.

GARY: (pressing by) That's great. Don't mind me. I'll only be a few minutes.

Analysis

1. How should Pastor Dan handle the situation with Gary right now?
2. What effect is this interruption likely to have on Pastor Dan and Terri's evening? What long-term effect would you expect in their relationship? What long-term effect would you expect in their attitude toward the church?
3. Short of not living in a parsonage, how can pastors avoid such situations?

To summarize, the five most prevalent pitfalls to family communication include

1. Fatigue and time pressure
2. Financial pressure
3. Faulty expectations
4. Frequent moves
5. Fishbowl existence

Considering the impact of these five pitfalls to pastoral family communication, it is a wonder that quality family life exists at all among the clergy. Yet indications reveal that in spite of the difficulties, pastoral families are doing reasonably well.

Lee and Balswick (1989), after a careful examination of pastoral families, conclude, "Thus we find no basis for believing that clergy families are generally in trouble" (p. 270). McBurney (1985) declares, "PKs are an amazing group. They have special grace, I'm convinced; they put up with an awful lot of stress and abuse from congregations as well as neglect from their minister parents. Yet they seem to emerge committed to Christ" (p. 116).

One reason for this resilience is that pastoral families are not helpless victims of the stress of pastoral ministry. Pastoral family members usually recognize their responsibility to one another, and are able to overcome the difficulties. In fact, many come to recognize that they have some unique and tremendous resources to aid them in establishing quality family communication.

RESOURCES FOR PASTORAL FAMILY COMMUNICATION

Pastoral families have the same vast assortment of family helps available that any other family might use to combat pitfalls to family communication. In addition, pastoral families usually benefit from three important resources that are unique to their situation.

Breadth of Friendships

The flip side of the frequent moves coin is that pastoral families have available to them a host of friendships and acquaintances in a variety of settings (Hobkirk, 1961). These friendships can provide a great source of encouragement and resources for wholeness when the communication pitfalls threaten family stability.

Sometimes another pastor friend becomes the resource. In one pastoral family the pressures of adolescence led to open rebellion against family standards. A colleague from a distant city who had been very influential in the young person's earlier life proved to be the key to healing. He voluntarily traveled many miles to sit down with the PK in friend-to-friend counseling. The results were phenomenal.

In other cases, the friendship of laypeople provides the resources necessary to overcome pitfalls to family communication. Pastors who have been in the profession for more than a few years will usually know at least one resource in a variety of professions. Often this breadth of friendships can be utilized to assist in overcoming the pitfalls to pastoral family communication.

For example, one pastor was faced with the need for more reliable transportation in spite of already overwhelming financial pressures. Before the pressures led to a breakdown of healthy family communication between the pastor and his spouse, a friend from a former parish, who operated an automobile dealership, was consulted. This former parishioner was able to find an affordable automobile that met the needs of the pastoral family. As noted in Chapter 13, returning to a former parish for any reason raises serious ethical questions. Thus, in cases such as this one, it is important to consult with the current pastor and also to avoid any communication or activity that may be viewed as pastoral in nature.

In another situation a parsonage family was feeling intensely the pressures of the fishbowl. A friend from another community, with whom the pastor had become acquainted at a denominational meeting, made his lake cottage available for a week of rest and relaxation. The results in improved pastoral family communication were incredibly positive. The breadth of relationship resource made the brief escape possible.

Built-In Support Group

A second resource available to the pastoral family as they endeavor to overcome the pitfalls of pastoral family communication is the built-in support group that comes from being an integral part of a local church congregation. Lee and Balswick (1989) point out that "when the minister's family can feel the love and support of church members, family life is made easier" (p. 202). They base that conclusion on their study showing that the more integrated a pastoral family is into a congregation, the lower the family's feelings of stress. Sadly, many pastors develop an "us against them" mentality with regard to the very people they are called to love and shepherd. This mentality not only reduces their effectiveness but robs their family of an important resource in the fight against communication pitfalls.

A young pastor named Chad reported recently that he had sought and been granted a move to a different congregation by his denominational officials. "It really came a year too late," he lamented. Pastor Chad recalled that the former church "wouldn't come around to my way of doing things. In addition," he continued, "they insisted on taking potshots at my children."

Although it is difficult and perhaps dangerous to analyze a pastor-parish relationship on the basis of such scant information, several facts do emerge.

1. Pastor Chad believes the church should do things his way rather than he discovering their long-term approach to ministry.
2. Pastor Chad never became integrated into the life of the congregation.
3. Pastor Chad became understandably defensive when the regressive spiral relationship between he and the church began to impact his family.

Pastor Chad may have intentionally distanced himself from the congregation. Many pastors believe that their position of authority is eroded if they get too close to the people they serve. "One way to avoid this erosion of authority is to construct a system of walls around oneself. Unfortunately those protective barriers also isolate" (McBurney, 1977, p. 61). In addition, they rob the pastor's family of the built-in support group available to more well-integrated pastoral families.

Bilateral Call

Many pastors believe that the pressures and stresses of pastoral ministry are so intense that they should not be undertaken except by a clear and compelling call of God. They contend that along with God's call comes God's grace to help meet the demands. Many pastors and researchers into pastoral ministry are discovering that a joint sense of call by both a pastor and a pastor's spouse provides a powerful resource against the breakdown of communication within the family.

Nelson (1977) explores the concept of bilateral call. She offers keen insight into what the spouses of pastors can expect from ministry and what demands will be placed upon them. Supporting the notion of a shared call, she writes to pastor's spouses, "If we are to survive the claims of a demanding world, it is essential that we develop a strong sense of personal responsibility to God" (Nelson, 1977, p. 42).

For those 65 percent of pastoral spouses who knew at the time of marriage that they were marrying a minister, the bilateral call is more easily discerned (Mickey and Ashmore, 1991, p. 72). When the partner did not know the spouse would enter a career in ministry, the couple should proceed as a team and develop or recognize the call together.

Some evidence also suggests that developing that sense of call within pastoral children assists in keeping the whole family's lines of communication open.

> The more clearly the call is discerned by the pastor and the more thoroughly the decision is processed by the family, the higher the level of support for ministry and the less likely the family is to be harshly surprised by the realities of ministry. (Mickey and Ashmore, 1991, p. 72)

In one pastoral family, the expectation of the congregation that the pastor entertain overnight visiting missionaries and evangelists could have become a pitfall to family communication. The problem was intensified since the size of the parsonage made it necessary for an elementary-age PK to give up her bedroom in favor of the living room sofa. When the resource of bilateral call was employed, however, the matter was satisfactorily resolved. The pastor/parent used the occasion to explain the nature of Christian service and to challenge, "Honey, God is asking you to make your ministry giving up your space for the missionaries." The child let the whole church as well as friends at school know about her special "call." Twenty years later, that particular pastoral family celebrates the long-term outcome. The child, now a young adult, has recently responded along with her husband to a call to become a career missionary in Africa.

This success story is not unique. Many pastoral families are overcoming the pitfalls by employing their unique resources in the battle to achieve effective family communication. The process is not easy. In fact, most pastoral families discover it is downright demanding, but the results make the effort worthwhile.

KEY CONCEPTS

The single most important interpersonal relationship of a pastor is his or her immediate family. Pastoral families live within a social context that makes effective family communication challenging. Among the pitfalls to effective family communication are:

- Fatigue and time pressure
- Financial pressure
- Faulty expectations
- Frequent moves
- Fishbowl existence

On the positive side, however, pastoral families have many resources available for dealing with the pitfalls. These resources are more plentiful in a pastoral ministry setting than in most other professional situations. These resources include

- Breadth of friendships
- Built-in support groups
- Bilateral call

MEANINGS MANIA

Word Bank

a. royal family complex
b. bilateral call
c. breadth of friendship

Definitions

_____ 1. Provides a lot of friends in a lot of places
_____ 2. Provides love and respect solely on the basis of profession
_____ 3. Sensed by more than one member of a family

UNLEASHING THE POWER
OF INTERPERSONAL COMMUNICATION

Conduct an interview with an adult who grew up as the son or daughter of a pastor. What does the interviewee see as the unique challenges of being a PK? What are the greatest advantages? What one thing could a pastoral parent do to make growing up less stressful?

Conduct an interview with a pastoral spouse. How does the spouse view his or her role? Is the concept of bilateral call important to the interviewee? How difficult is the fishbowl existence? What are the greatest pressures of pastoral family life? What are the greatest resources?

References

Adler, Ronald B. and Neil Towne (2003). *Looking Out/Looking In,* Tenth edition. Belmont, CA: Wadsworth/Thomson Learning.

Alberts, Jess K. and Yvonne Kellar-Guenther (1996). That's not funny: Understanding recipients' responses to teasing, *Western Journal of Communication* 60(4): 337-357.

Anderson, Carole Broussen (1998). The experience of growing up in a minister's home and the religious commitment of the adult child of a minister, *Pastoral Psychology* 46(6): 393-412.

Andrews, Patricia H. and John E. Baird (2000). *Communication for Business and the Professions,* Seventh edition. Boston: McGraw-Hill.

Argyle, Michael (1990). *Bodily Communication,* Second edition. New York: Routledge.

Aristotle. *On Rhetoric.* Trans. G. A. Kennedy (1991). Oxford: Oxford University Press.

Asch, Solomon (1946). Forming impressions of personality, *Journal of Abnormal and Social Psychology* 41(3): 258-290.

Augsburger, David (1981). *Caring Enough to Forgive / Caring Enough to Not Forgive.* Ventura, CA: Regal.

Auslander, Gail K. and Howard Litwin (1995). Social networks, social support, and self ratings of health among the elderly, *Journal of Aging and Health* 3(4): 493-510.

Barna, George (1990). *The Frog in the Kettle.* Ventura, CA: Regal.

———— (1993). *Today's Pastors.* Ventura, CA: Regal.

Baron, Penny (1974). Self-esteem, ingratiation, and evaluation of unknown others, *Journal of Personality and Social Psychology* 30(1): 104-109.

BBC News (2002). Rural isolation may cause diabetes, September 5, p. Health 1.

Beebe, Steven A., Susan J. Beebe, and Diana K. Ivy (2001). *Communication Principles for a Lifetime.* Boston: Allyn and Bacon.

Belz, Joel (2002). CEO's in the mirror, *World,* November 16, p. 5.

Berlo, David (1960). *The Process of Communication.* New York: Holt, Rinehart, and Winston.

Blau, Peter M. (1964). *Exchange and Power in Social Life.* New York: John Wiley and Sons.

Borchers, Timothy A. (2002). *Persuasion in the Media Age.* Boston: McGraw-Hill.

Borisoff, Deborah and David A. Victor (1989). *Conflict Management: A Communication Skills Approach.* Englewood Cliffs, NJ: Prentice Hall.

Bouma, Mary LaGrand (1981). Pastors' kids, ministering children, *Leadership* 2(4): 30-38.

Bradbury, Thomas N. and Frank D. Fincham (1990). Attributions in marriage: Review and critique, *Psychological Bulletin* 107(1): 3-33.

Brown, Daniel A. with Brian Larson (1976). *The Other Side of Pastoral Ministry: Using Process Leadership to Transform Your Church.* Grand Rapids, MI: Zondervan.

Burgoon, Judee K. (1994). Nonverbal signals. In Knapp, Mark L. and Gerald R. Miller (ed.), *Handbook of Interpersonal Communication,* Second edition (pp. 229-285). Thousand Oaks, CA: Sage.

Burke, Kenneth (1969). *A Rhetoric of Motives.* Berkley: University of California Press.

Burns, Jim (2003). *The 10 Building Blocks for a Happy Family.* Ventura CA: Regal.

Canary, Daniel J. and Laura Stafford, eds. (1993). *Communication and Relational Maintenance.* San Diego, CA: Academic Press.

Cannon, Angie (2003). Soaring college costs have millions of students earning a degree in debt, *Readers Digest,* November, pp. 96-103.

Chirban, John T. (1994). When clergy sexual abuse occurs. In Chirban, John T. (ed.), *Clergy Sexual Misconduct: Orthodox Christian Perspectives* (pp. 47-64). Brookline, MA: Hellenic College.

Clinton, Timothy and George Ohlschlager, eds. (2002). *Competent Christian Counseling: Foundations and Practice of Compassionate Soul Care,* Volume I. Colorado Springs, CO: Waterbook Press.

Cloud, Henry and John Townsend (1992). *Boundaries.* Grand Rapids, MI: Zondervan.

———— (2003). *Boundaries Face to Face.* Grand Rapids, MI: Zondervan.

Cohen, Claudia E. (1983). Inferring the characteristics of other people: Categories and attribute accessibility, *Journal of Personality and Social Psychology* 44(1): 34-44.

Cohen, Sheldon (1981). Sound effects on behavior, *Psychology Today,* October, pp. 38-49.

Collins, Gary R. (1990). *Excellence and Ethics in Counseling.* Waco, TX: Word.

Collins, Sandra D. (2005). *Managing Conflict and Workplace Relationships.* Volume 5 in O'Rourke, James S. IV (ed.), *Managerial Communication Series.* Mason, OH: Thomson South-Western.

Conville, Richard (1991). *Relational Transitions: The Evolution of Personal Relationships.* New York: Praeger.

Cool, Lisa Collier (2004). The power of forgiving, *Readers Digest,* May, pp. 90-95.

Coser, Lewis A. (1956). *The Functions of Social Conflict.* Glencoe, IL: The Free Press.

Countryman, L. William (1998). *Forgiven and Forgiving.* Harrisburg, PA: Morehouse.

Coyle, Catherine T. and Robert D. Enright (1997). Forgiveness intervention with postabortion men, *Journal of Consulting and Clinical Psychology* 65(6): 1042-1046.

Cozby, Paul C. (1973). Self-disclosure: A literature review, *Psychological Bulletin* 79(2): 73-91.

Cross, Gary P., Jean H. Names, and Darrell Beck (1979). *Conflict and Human Interaction.* Dubuque, IA: Kendall Hunt.

Derlega, Valerian J. and Janusz Grzelak (1979). Appropriateness of self-disclosure. In Chelune, Gordon J. (ed.), *Self-Disclosure: Origins, Patterns, and Implications of Openness in Interpersonal Relationships* (pp. 151-176). San Francisco: Jossey-Bass.

DeVito, Joseph A. (1990). *Messages: Building Interpersonal Communication Skills.* New York: Harper and Row.

———— (1998). *The Interpersonal Communication Book,* Eighth edition. New York: Longman.

———— (2000). *Human Communication: The Basic Course,* Eighth edition. New York: Longman.

Donohue, William A. and Robert Kolt (1992). *Managing Interpersonal Conflict.* Newbury Park, CA: Sage.

Douglas, William (1961). Minister and wife: Growth in relationship, *Pastoral Psychology* 12(119): 35-39.

Drakeford, John W. (1982). *The Awesome Power of the Listening Heart.* Grand Rapids, MI: Zondervan.

Duncan, King with Rebecca Clark (1996). *The One-Minute Motivator.* Knoxville, TN: Seven Worlds Corp.

Edward, Gene (1994). *Crucified by Christians.* Beumont, TX: Seedsowers.

Edwards, Renee and Richard Bello (2001). The effects of loneliness and verbal aggressiveness on message interpretation, *Southern Communication Journal* 66(2): 139-150.

Ekman, Paul and Wallace V. Friesen (1969). The repertoire of nonverbal behavior: Categories, origins, usage, and coding, *Semeotica* 1(1): 49-98.

———— (1975). *Unmasking the Face.* Englewood Cliffs, NJ: Prentice Hall.

Emmons, Michael and David Richardson (1981). *The Assertive Christian.* San Francisco: Harper and Row.

Festinger, Leon (1962). *A Theory of Cognitive Dissonance.* Stanford, CA: Stanford University Press.

Fisher, B. Aubrey (1974). *Small Group Decision Making.* New York: McGraw-Hill.

Fisher, Roger, William Ury, and Bruce Patton (1991). *Getting to Yes: Negotiating Agreement Without Giving In,* Second edition. New York: Penguin Books.

Fotheringham, Wallace C. (1966). *Perspectives on Persuasion.* Boston: Allyn and Bacon.

Freedman, Suzanne R. and Robert D. Enright (1996). Forgiveness as an intervention goal with incest survivors, *Journal of Consulting and Clinical Psychology* 64(5): 983-992.

French, John R.P. Jr. and Bertram Raven (1968). The basis of social power. In Cartwright, Dorwin and Alvin Zander (eds.), *Group Dynamics: Research and Theory,* Third edition (pp. 259-269). New York: Harper and Row.

Gilbert, Shirley J. (1976). Empirical and theoretical extensions of self-disclosure. In Miller, Gerald R. (ed.), *Explorations in Interpersonal Communication* (pp. 197-216). Beverly Hills, CA: Sage.

Graham, Franklin (1995). *Rebel with a Cause.* Nashville: Thomas Nelson.

Greenberg, Leslie S., Laura N. Rice, and Robert Elliott (1993). *Facilitating Emotional Change: The Moment-by-Moment Process.* New York: Guilford.

Griffin, Em (1987). *Making Friends and Making Them Count.* Downers Grove, IL: Inter-Varsity.

――― (2003). *A First Look at Communication Theory,* Fifth edition. Boston: McGraw-Hill.

Guerra, Alberto (2001). Keep it faithful, *Leadership* 22(2): 57-61.

Gula, Richard M. (1996). *Ethics in Pastoral Ministry.* New York: Paulist.

Gwinn, Ralph A. (2001). *Restoring Relationships: The Importance of Forgiving and Being Forgiven.* Hagerstown, MD: Fairmont.

Hahn, Todd (2001). Keep it real, *Leadership* 22(2): 59-61.

Hall, Edward T. (1966). *The Hidden Dimension.* Garden City, NJ: Doubleday.

Hall, Madelyn and Betty Havens (2001). The effects of social isolation and loneliness on the health of older women, *Center of Excellence for Women's Health Research Bulletin* 2(2): 3-23.

Harley, Willard F. Jr. (2001). *His Needs, Her Needs: Building an Affair-Proof Marriage.* Grand Rapids: Revell.

Harris, John C. (1977). *Stress, Power, and Ministry.* Washington, DC: The Albian Institute.

Hart, Archibald (1982). Transference: Loosening the tie that binds, *Leadership* 3(4): 110-117.

Hatcher, Wayne (1986). Learning to listen before we speak, *Church Administration,* March, p. 18.

Haug, Ingeborg E. (1999). Boundaries and the use and misuse of power and authority: Ethical complexities for clergy psychotherapists, *Journal of Counseling and Development,* 77(4): 411.

Healey, Bede J. (1990). Self-disclosure in religious spiritual direction: Antecedents and parallels to self-disclosure in psychology. In Stricker, George and Martin Fisher (eds.), *Self-Disclosure in the Therapeutic Relationship* (pp. 17-30). New York: Plenum Press.

Heider, Fritz (1946). Attitudes and cognitive organization, *Journal of Psychology* 21(1): 107-112.

――― (1958). *Psychology of Interpersonal Relations.* New York: Wiley and Sons.

Hickman, Martha L. and Don W. Stacks (1993). *Nonverbal Communication Studies and Application.* Madison, WI: Brown and Benchmark.

Hill, Clara E. and Karen M. O'Brien (1999). *Helping Skills: Facilitating Exploration, Insight, and Action.* Washington, DC: American Psychological Association.

Hobkirk, Marietta B. (1961). Some reflections on bringing up the minister's family, *Pastoral Psychology* 12(119): 25-30.

Holy Bible: New International Version (1973/1978/1984). Grand Rapids, MI: Zondervan.

Honstead, Mary (2004). Leading an interesting private life (when your public life is ministry), *Circuit Rider* 28(1): 13.

Huang, Shih-Tsent Tina and Robert D. Enright (2000). Forgiveness and anger related emotions in Taiwan: Implications for therapy, *Psychotherapy: Theory, Research, Practice, Training* 37(1): 71-79.

Insel, Paul M. and Lenore F. Jacobson, eds. (1975). *What Do You Expect? An Inquiry into Self-Fulfilling Prophecies.* Menlo Park, CA: Cummings.

Jenco, Lawrence Martin (1995). *Bound to Forgive: The Pilgrimage to Reconciliation of a Beirut Hostage.* Notre Dame, IN: Ave Maria.

Johannesen, Richard (2002). *Ethics in Human Communication,* Fifth edition. Prospect Heights, IL: Waveland.

Johnson, David W. (1997). *Reaching Out: Interpersonal Effectiveness and Self-Actualization,* Sixth edition. Boston, MA: Allyn and Bacon.

Jones, Edward E. and Keith E. Davis (1965). From acts to dispositions: The attribution process in person perception. In Berkowitz, Leonard (ed.), *Advances in Experimental Social Psychology,* Volume 2 (pp. 219-266). New York: Academic Press.

Jones, Stanley and A. Elaine Yarbrough (1985). A naturalistic study of the meanings of touch, *Communication Monographs* 52(1): 19-56.

Jourard, Sydney M. (1971). *The Transparent Self.* New York: D. Van Nostrand.

Kagle, Jill Doner and Pam Northrup Geibelhausen (1994). Dual relationships and professional boundaries, *Social Work* 39(2): 213-221.

Karren, Keith J., Brent Q. Hafen, N. Lee Smith, and Kathryn J. Frandsen (2002). *Mind/Body Health: The Effects of Attitudes, Emotions and Relationships,* Second edition. Redwood City, CA: Benjamin Cummings.

Kazavorich, Lisa Hurt (2001). Residents complain of illness, cite factory hum, *The Kokomo Tribune,* July 17, p. A1.

Ketterman, Grace and David Hazard (2000). *When You Can't Say, "I Forgive You": Breaking the Bonds of Anger and Hurt.* Colorado Springs, CO: NavPress.

Kilmann, Ralph H. and Kenneth W. Thomas (1975). Interpersonal conflict—Handling behavior as reflections of Jungian personality dimensions, *Psychological Reports* 37(3): 971-980.

Knapp, Mark L. (1978). *Social Intercourse.* Boston: Allyn and Bacon.

Kohn, Alfie (1988). Girl talk, guy talk, *Psychology Today,* February, pp. 65-66.

Krebs, Richard (1980). Why pastors should not be counselors, *The Journal of Pastoral Care,* 34(4): 229-233.

Krivanek, Patricia Schileppi (2000). *How Then Shall We Live?* New York: McGraw-Hill.

Laing, Milli (1993). Gossip: Does it play a role in the socialization of nurses? *Journal of Nursing Scholarship* 25(1): 37-43.

Larson, Charles U. (2004). *Persuasion: Reception and Responsibility,* Tenth edition. Belmont, CA: Wadsworth/Thomson Learning.

Laswell, Thomas E. and Marcia E. Laswell (1976). I love you, but I'm not in love with you, *Journal of Marriage and Family Counseling* 2(2): 211-224.

Lavender, Lucille (1986). *They Cry Too: Pastors Don't Belong on Pedestals.* Grand Rapids, MI: Zondervan.

Lee, Cameron (1992). *Helping Pastors' Kids Through Their Identity Crisis.* Grand Rapids, MI: Zondervan.

Lee, Cameron and Jack Balswick (1989). *Life in a Glass House: The Minister's Family in Its Unique Social Context.* Grand Rapids, MI: Zondervan.

Levinson, Daniel J. (1978). *The Seasons of a Man's Life.* New York: Ballantine.

Lewis, Beverly (1997). *The Shunning.* Minneapolis, MN: Bethany House.

Lewis, G. Douglas (1981). *Resolving Church Conflicts.* San Francisco: Harper and Row.

Luft, Joseph (1969). *Of Human Interaction.* Palo Alto, CA: National Press.

Marshall, Evan (1983). *Eye Language: Understanding the Eloquent Eye.* New York: New Trend.

Maslow, Abraham H. (1970). *Motivation and Personality.* New York: Harper and Row.

May, Rollo (1972). *Power and Innocence.* New York: W.W. Norton.

McBurney, Louis (1977). *Every Pastor Needs a Pastor.* Waco, TX: Word.

———— (1985). Reflections. In Merrill, Dean (ed.), *Clergy Couples in Crisis: The Impact of Stress on Pastoral Marriages* (pp. 67-70). Waco, TX: Word.

McCullough, Michael E., Steven J. Sandage, and Everett L. Worthington Jr. (1997). *To Forgive Is Human.* Downers Grove, IL: Intervarsity.

McDaniel, Eugene B. with James L. Johnson (1975). *Before Honor.* Philadelphia: A.J. Holman.

McKeever, Joe (2001). Broken pastor, broken church, *Leadership* 22(1): 57-64.

McSwain, Larry L. and William C. Treadwell Jr. (1989). *Conflict Ministry in the Church.* Nashville: Broadman.

Meier, Paul D., Frank B. Minirth, Frank B. Wichern, and Donald E. Ratcliff (1991). *Introduction to Psychology and Counseling.* Grand Rapids, MI: Baker.

Michaud, Ellen (1999). Discover the power of forgiveness, *Prevention,* January, p. 110.

Mickey, Paul A. and Ginny W. Ashmore (1991). *Clergy Families: Is Normal Life Possible?* Grand Rapids, MI: Zondervan.

Montgomery, Marilyn J. and Camille DeBell (1997). Dual relationships and pastoral counseling: Asset and liability, *Counseling and Values* 42(1): 30-41.

Montgomery, Robert L. (1981). *Listening Made Easy: How To Improve Listening on the Job, at Home, and in the Community.* New York: Amacom.

Morrow, Lance (1984). I spoke . . . as a brother, *Time,* January 9, pp. 27-33.

Mulac, Anthony, John M. Wiemann, Sally J. Widenmann, and Toni W. Gibson (1988). Male/female language differences and effects in same-sex and mixed-sex dyads, *Communication Monographs* 55(4): 315-339.

Neff, Blake J. (1995). Family communication. In Neff, Blake J. and Donald Ratcliff (eds.), *Handbook of Family Religious Education* (pp. 137-163). Birmingham, AL: Religious Education Press.

Nelson, Martha (1977). *This Call We Share.* Nashville: Broadman.

Newcomb, Theodore M. (1961). *The Acquaintance Process.* New York: Holt, Rinehart, and Winston.

Nicholi, Armand M. Jr. (1985). Commitment to the family. In Rekers, George (ed.), *Family Building: Six Qualities of a Strong Family* (pp. 51-66). Ventura, CA: Regal.

Nichols, Michael P. (1995). *The Lost Art of Listening.* New York: Guilford.

Oates, Wayne E., ed. (1959). *An Introduction to Pastoral Counseling.* Nashville: Broadman.

Ochroch, Ruth S. (1987). The pastor—psychologist: An unethical dual relationship? *Journal of Pastoral Counseling* 22(1): 17-23.

Orr, Tamra B. (2002). Assert yourself!, *Current Health* 28(5): 18.

Osgood, Charles E. and Percy H. Tannenbaum (1955). The principle of congruity in the prediction of attitude change, *Psychological Review* 62(1): 42-55.

Palmer, Mark T. (1989). Controling conversations: Turns, topics, and interpersonal control, *Communication Monographs* 56(1): 1-18.

Pearson, Linda J. (2003). Our ethical boundaries and dilemmas, *The Nurse Practitioner* 28(2): 4.

Piaget, Jean (1954). *Construction of Reality in the Child.* New York: Basic.

Pietrofesa, John J., Cathy J. Pietrofesa, and John D. Pietrofesa (1990). The mental health counselor and "duty to warn," *Journal of Mental Health Counseling* 12(2): 129-137.

Powell, John S. J. (1969). *Why am I Afraid to Tell You Who I Am?* Niles, IL: Argue Communications.

Rainer, Thom S. (2001). *Surprising Insights from the Unchurched and Proven Ways to Reach Them.* Grand Rapids, MI: Zondervan.

Rainey, Dennis, ed. (2002). *Building Strong Families.* Wheaton, IL: Crossway.

Ratcliff, Donald (1995). Parenting and religious education. In Neff, Blake J. and Donald Ratcliff (eds.), *Handbook of Family Religious Education* (pp. 61-86). Birmingham, AL: Religious Education Press.

Reinland, Martin and Tricia S. Jones (1995). Interpersonal distance, body orientation and touch: Effects of culture, gender, and age, *Journal of Social Psychology* 135(3): 281-298.

Reinsch, Lamar N. and Annette N. Shelby (1999). What communication abilities do practioners need?: Evidence from MBA schools, *Business Communication Quarterly* 60(4): 7-29.

Rekers, George, ed. (1985). *Family Building: Six Qualities of a Strong Family.* Ventura, CA: Regal.

Richmond, Virginia P. and James C. McCroskey (2000). *Nonverbal Behavior in Interpersonal Relations,* Fourth edition. Boston: Allyn and Bacon.

Roach, Carol Ashburn and Nancy J. Wyatt (1988). *Successful Listening.* New York: Harper & Row.

Rokeach, Milton (1973). *The Nature of Human Values.* New York: Free Press.

Rosenfield, Lawrence B. (1979). Self-disclosure avoidance: Why am I afraid to tell you who I am? *Communication Monographs* 46(1): 63-74.

Sande, Ken (2004). *The Peace Maker: A Biblical Guide to Resolving Personal Conflict.* Grand Rapids, MI: Baker.

Saxe, John Godfrey (1852). *Poems.* Boston: Ticknor, Reed, and Fields.

Seamands, David (1981). *Healing for Damaged Emotions.* Wheaton, IL: Victor.

——— (1995). *If Only.* Wheaton, IL: Victor.

Seamands, David and Helen Seamands (1981). The story of raising a pastoral family: An interview with David and Helen Seamands, *Leadership* 2(4): 16-28.

Sheldon, William H. (1940). *The Varieties of Human Physique.* New York: Harper and Brothers.

Sherif, Mazafer, Carolyn Sherif, and Roger Nebergall (1965). *Attitude and Attitude Change: The Social Judgment-Involvement Approach.* Philadelphia: W. B. Saunder.

Sias, Patricia M. (1996). Constructing perceptions of differential treatment: An analysis of coworker discourse, *Communication Monographs* 63(2): 171-187.

Simons, Herbert W. (1972). Persuasion in social conflicts: A critique of prevailing conceptions and a framework for future research, *Speech Monographs* 39(4): 227-247.

Smoke, Jim (2004). *7 Keys to a Healthy Blended Family.* Eugene, OR: Harvest House.

Sommer, Robert (1959). Studies in personal space, *Sociometry* 22(3): 247-260.

Stafford, Tim (2004). *Never Mind the Joneses.* Downers Grove, IL: InterVarsity.

Stanton, Glenn T. (2004). *My Crazy Imperfect Christian Family: Living Out Your Faith with Those Who Know You Best.* Colorado Springs, CO: NavPress.

Stewart, John, ed. (1973). *Bridges not Walls.* Reading, MA: Addison-Wesley.

Stowell, Joe (2001). Keep it on Christ in you, *Leadership* 22(2): 59.

Switzer, David K. (1983). Why pastors should be counselors (of a sort): A response to Richard L. Krebs, *The Journal of Pastoral Care* 37(1): 28-32.

Tannen, Deborah (1990). *You Just Don't Understand Women and Men in Conversation.* New York: William Morrow.

———— (1994). *Talking from 9 To 5: Women and Men in the Workplace: Language, Sex, and Power.* New York: William Morrow.

Taylor, Richard S. (1989). *Principles of Pastoral Success.* Grand Rapids, MI: Zondervan.

Thompson, Wayne N. (1975). *The Process of Persuasion: Principles and Readings.* New York: Harper and Row.

Tiemann, William Harold and John C. Bush (1983). *The Right to Silence: Privileged Clergy Communication and the Law.* Nashville: Abingdon.

Tuckman, Bruce W. (1965). Developmental sequence in small groups, *Psychological Bulletin* 63(6): 384-399.

Vangelisti, Anita L., Mark L. Knapp, and John A. Daly (1990). Conversational narcissism, *Communication Monographs* 57(4): 251-274.

Vanleer, C. Arthur Jr. (1987). The formation of social relationships: A longitudinal study of social penetration, *Human Communication Research* 13(1): 314.

Veenendall, Thomas L. and Marjorie C. Feinstein (1996). *Lets Talk About Relationships: Cases in Study,* Second edition. Prospect Heights, IL: Waveland Press.

Veroff, Joseph, Richard A. Kulka, and Elizabeth Ann Malcolm Douvan (1981). *Mental Health in America.* New York: Basic.

Watzlawick, Paul, Janet H. Beavin, and Don D. Jackson (1967). *Pragmatics of Human Communication.* New York: W. W. Norton.

Weaver, Andrew J. and Harold G. Koenig (1997). Marriage and family therapists and the clergy: A need for clinical collaboration, training, and research, *Journal of Marital and Family Therapy* 23(1): 13-27.

Weaver, Carl H. (1972). *Human Listening: Processes and Behavior.* Indianapolis, IN: Bobbs-Merrill.

Weaver, Richard L. (1996). *Understanding Interpersonal Communication,* Seventh edition. New York: Longman.

Wells, Bob (2004). The place of friendship in ministry, *Circuit Rider* 28(1): 16.

Whorf, Benjamin L. and John B. Carroll (1998). *Language, Thought, and Reality: Selected Writings of Benjamin Lee Whorf.* Cambridge: Massachusetts Institute of Technology.

Williams, Redford B. and Margaret A. Chesney (1993). Psychosocial factors and prognosis in established coronary heart disease, *Journal of American Medical Association* 270(15): 1860-1861.

Wilmot, William W. and Joyce L. Hocker (2001). *Interpersonal Conflict,* Sixth edition. Boston, MA: McGraw-Hill.

Witvliet, Charlotte vanoyen (2001). Forgiveness and health: Review and reflections on a matter of faith, feelings, and physiology, *Journal of Psychology and Theology* 29(3): 212-224.

Witvliet, Charlotte vanoyen, Thomas Ludwig, and Kelly Vander Laan (2001). Granting forgiveness or harboring grudges: Implications for emotion, physiology, and health, *Psychological Science* 12(2): 117-123.

Wolvin, Andrew and Carolyn Gwynn Coakley (1996). *Listening,* Fifth edition. Madison: Brown and Benchmark.

Wood, Julia T. (2005). *Gendered Lives: Communication, Gender, and Culture,* Sixth edition. Belmont, CA: ThomsonWadsworth.

Woodward, Kenneth L. (1995). Religion: To forgive is human, too, *Newsweek,* January 16, p. 62.

Wynn, John Charles (1960). Pastors have family problems too, *Pastoral Psychology* 11(106): 7-10.

Index

('i' indicates an illustration)

Order a copy of this book with this form or online at:
http://www.haworthpress.com/store/product.asp?sku=5388

A PASTOR'S GUIDE TO INTERPERSONAL COMMUNICATION
The Other Six Days

_____ in hardbound at $39.95 (ISBN-13: 978-0-7890-2665-1; ISBN-10: 0-7890-2665-1)

_____ in softbound at $24.95 (ISBN-13: 978-0-7890-2666-8; ISBN-10: 0-7890-2666-X)

Or order online and use special offer code HEC25 in the shopping cart.

COST OF BOOKS_____

☐ **BILL ME LATER:** (Bill-me option is good on US/Canada/Mexico orders only; not good to jobbers, wholesalers, or subscription agencies.)

☐ Check here if billing address is different from shipping address and attach purchase order and billing address information.

POSTAGE & HANDLING_____
(US: $4.00 for first book & $1.50 for each additional book)
(Outside US: $5.00 for first book & $2.00 for each additional book)

Signature_____

SUBTOTAL_____

☐ **PAYMENT ENCLOSED: $**_____

IN CANADA: ADD 7% GST_____

☐ **PLEASE CHARGE TO MY CREDIT CARD.**

STATE TAX_____
(NJ, NY, OH, MN, CA, IL, IN, PA, & SD residents, add appropriate local sales tax)

☐ Visa ☐ MasterCard ☐ AmEx ☐ Discover
☐ Diner's Club ☐ Eurocard ☐ JCB

Account # _____

FINAL TOTAL_____
(If paying in Canadian funds, convert using the current exchange rate, UNESCO coupons welcome)

Exp. Date_____

Signature_____

Prices in US dollars and subject to change without notice.

NAME_____

INSTITUTION_____

ADDRESS_____

CITY_____

STATE/ZIP_____

COUNTRY_____ COUNTY (NY residents only)_____

TEL_____ FAX_____

E-MAIL_____

May we use your e-mail address for confirmations and other types of information? ☐ Yes ☐ No
We appreciate receiving your e-mail address and fax number. Haworth would like to e-mail or fax special discount offers to you, as a preferred customer. **We will never share, rent, or exchange your e-mail address or fax number.** We regard such actions as an invasion of your privacy.

Order From Your Local Bookstore or Directly From
The Haworth Press, Inc.
10 Alice Street, Binghamton, New York 13904-1580 • USA
TELEPHONE: 1-800-HAWORTH (1-800-429-6784) / Outside US/Canada: (607) 722-5857
FAX: 1-800-895-0582 / Outside US/Canada: (607) 771-0012
E-mail to: orders@haworthpress.com

For orders outside US and Canada, you may wish to order through your local sales representative, distributor, or bookseller.
For information, see http://haworthpress.com/distributors

(Discounts are available for individual orders in US and Canada only, not booksellers/distributors.)

PLEASE PHOTOCOPY THIS FORM FOR YOUR PERSONAL USE.
http://www.HaworthPress.com   BOF06